THE MOUNTAINS OF PARIS

The Mountains of Paris

HOW AWE AND WONDER REWROTE MY LIFE

David Oates

Oregon State University Press   Corvallis

Library of Congress Cataloging-in-Publication Data

Names: Oates, David, 1950– author.
Title: The mountains of Paris : how awe and wonder rewrote my life / David Oates.
Description: Corvallis OR : Oregon State University Press, 2019. | Includes bibliographical
    references.
Identifiers: LCCN 2019025123 | ISBN 9780870719813 (trade paperback)
Subjects: LCSH: Oates, David, 1950—Travel—France—Paris. | Paris (France)—Description
    and travel.
Classification: LCC PS3565.A78 Z46 2019 | DDC 811/.54 [B]—dc23
LC record available at https://lccn.loc.gov/2019025123

♾This paper meets the requirements of ANSI/NISO Z39.48-1992 (Permanence of Paper).

First published in 2019 by Oregon State University Press
Printed in the United States of America

Oregon State University Press
121 The Valley Library
Corvallis OR 97331-4501
541-737-3166 • fax 541-737-3170
www.osupress.oregonstate.edu

To Gwen Pacallet, *our best friend in France*
1956–2016

To Jean Guillou, *organist, Église Saint-Eustache de Paris*
1930–2019

Contents

terror visits
before beauty
the strange joy

l'epouvante fréquente
devant la beauté
l'etrange joie

—Franck André Jamme, *Au Secret*

We had the experience but missed the meaning

—T. S. Eliot, *Four Quartets*

Acknowledgments

Versions of some of these essays have appeared in:

Georgia Review (Summer 2018); *Seven Hills Review* (2018); *Soundings*, Northwest Institute of Literary Arts (Summer 2016); *Tiferet: Literature, Art, and Creative Spirit* (Fall 2016); *Wortschau* (in German and English), Düsseldorf, Germany, (October 2015); *Pooled Ink*, Northern Colorado Writers (2014)

Thanks to:

Cité internationale des arts, Paris: for my long sojourn as your guest, which allowed me the astounding privilege of open-ended walking, thinking, and writing, in the planet's greatest city (January–April 2014).

Tiferet: Literature, Art, and Creative Spirit: Nonfiction Prize (2016) for two chapters of this book.

Northern Colorado Writers Association: *Nonfiction Prize* (2014) for a chapter of this book.

Pushcart Prize: 2014 nonfiction essay nomination.

Seven Hills Review: *Nonfiction Award*, second place (2018) for a chapter of this book.

December: finalist, 2019 Curt Johnson Prose Award.

RACC Regional Arts and Culture Council, Portland: grant underwriting my process of clarification and discovery (2015).

Vermont Studio Center: for my writing residency and a grant underwriting part of my stay (May 2015), where this book took surprising shape beside the waters of the Gihon and the Lamoille.

Peregrine Literary Series: for the opportunity to read a chapter to a Portland audience (November 2014).

Personal thanks to:

Fellow writing residents at Vermont Studio Center: for your encouraging reception at readings of early chapters ("St Eustache #1,"" Voices")

Nonsox Writers Group, Portland: for your wise help with "Balthasar Denner, Bill Viola." Thanks also to Alex Hirsch and Linda Wysong for helpful readings of this chapter.

Andrea Hollander: for your love of what became "The Flatness," and for your general writerly help.

Dr. Dahlia Zaidel, UCLA Brain Research Institute: for your helpful responses to my "neuroaesthetics" queries.

Christine and Bob Hamilton-Pennell: for helpful readings of several chapters.

Dr. Seth White: for general encouragement and especially helpful feedback on science, rivers, and trout.

Impersonal thanks to:

Caféotheque, Paris: for inspiring space where the core imaginative work of this project originated (afternoons, 2:00).

Le Perle, Paris: for good beer and convivial public space perfect for reviewing the day's work (afternoons, 5:00).

The "Rameau" piano, *salle de répétition*, third floor, Cité des arts: for the beautiful pure tone and ringing harmonics of your tenor range.

Église Sainte-Eustache de Paris: for space, sound, music, and humanity.

Prologue: *The Night Walk [memnoir]*

By the time I reached the cemetery on its bluff south of town, the fog had disappeared and the beginnings of sunrise were lighting up the horizon. I had spent all night walking, praying, and crying. This was October in Santa Barbara, and the Santa Ana winds had raised night mists but left us warm, electric, on edge.

Walking and praying, all night. At some point, desperate for God's love, I had tried bashing my fists into a chain-link fence. Raising blood: that was good. But I noted—from a corner of the mind where I watched myself ironically, judgingly—that I had stopped at one good bloody knuckle.

Yet the desperation was real. I was one of the uncountable gay kids trapped in evangelical Christianity: trapped by my own stubbornness in not quitting the faith, trapped again by fear of rejection by my family and friends—above all trapped by fear of the degeneracy so confidently predicted for men, or boys, such as me. I was just twenty.

I saw the Pacific moving gray and silver all the way to its rim. At my feet was a long drop-off, rocks foaming in the surf. But despite my nightlong untethering, I felt no weepy self-extinction, no thought of making an end. No. There was just the seething, the power, the beauty.

I was standing in a grassy place with big oaks and pines, and I reached out to touch the rough moist bark of the nearest one. Laid my forehead there, catching the faint pine scent, sweet behind the salt mist. Felt something rushing, rushing, something bigger and truer than all this wailing and gnashing of teeth. Raised my eyes to look again.

Glow of pink and gold just beginning, bright planets still visible in the blue-violet sky, rightness and beauty all around me. Silent. Beyond doctrine. Greater than thought, and somehow welcoming in their indifference.

〰

I had no idea how to process what had just happened. Soon, or soon enough, I trudged back to campus, cleaned my face and squared my shoulders. A class in theology to prepare for (ours was a flyspeck Christian college, chosen for its earnestness). And then Survey of English Lit, something to read from the big thick Norton Anthology (Volume I). I'd get it done and have something to say for myself. Very determined about that.

I kept that morning in my heart, that glow, that rightness. But I also had a lifetime of God's alleged hate stored up in me, the unspoken contempt of family and church. I had been collecting these, silently watching and listening as people minced and mocked and joked, preached and misapplied Bible verses. Of course they had no idea about me; I knew how to pass. And they had meant well, meant to safeguard the flock, keep the children from the twisted ways of the world. We were cosseted, really: middle class kids in an uneventful corner of Los Angeles, dressed up for church, asked and warned and invited to follow the path of righteousness.

That's what I wanted, fiercely. I memorized, I prayed, I hid myself behind a barricade of vigilance and pretending. But it was hopeless. I was headed for misery, loneliness, perdition. Everyone in my world said so. And our pious college life wasn't changing anything.

Yet the morning world I saw, that seethe of beauty, that *extent* that went so much further than anything words could capture . . . I held that in my heart. It helped me see how small my story was, small and unremarkable. And for a second or a minute it healed me—silent on a cliff in California.

⚊

This big world—this immeasurable, wonderful, terrifying cosmos that we lose ourselves in, and find ourselves in—this is the subject of this book. The twilight all in fire and color. The night sky, limitless, incomprehensible. Even the strangeness of the living world—and of each other. What is it? What is this *tremendousness?* That breaks our heart with beauty, with longing, with fear and delight mixed so weirdly together? And that sometimes, unexpectedly, finds its echoes in the human arts—music especially and sometimes a painted canvas or some other handmade thing that again brings that note of endlessness, power, and beauty.

In the gradually blooming years that followed my sad night's journey, I strove unconsciously but continuously toward that undegenerate life I yearned for. It was a long time before I could handle other people—let alone the terrible question of love. So I headed for the mountains. At first with others, climbing and backpacking, but soon solo, solo for years and years. Years of stars rising over alpine basins and the clear, glowing granite of the

High Sierras. Years of riversides cloaked with welcoming pines and peaks walked or scrambled or climbed until the whole world unfurled before me. All of it indifferent, beautiful, and right. Slowly I believed it: that I might be right too. Small, yes. Lonely, yes. But right enough.

The story I told myself at first was the usual one: woe is me, suffering and hurt, and damn those narrow bigots. But all that dropped away in the mountains. Little by little the quieter, larger self grew. The wideness of the world was my tutor. It was beauty, it was scale, it was depth and complexity. All I had to do was keep silent and pay attention and absorb. Made small, I grew.

When I got to Paris so many decades later, I was finally ready to see it: that bigger story, deeper than hurt, wide as the sky.

Anyone could reenvision his or her story this way, I think. All it takes is remembering. And admitting: *Yes, it was beautiful, too. Savage . . . and beautiful.*

In Paris for a winter and the beginnings of a spring, I discovered a present so vivid—so full of art and music and people and life—that I began to rewrite my past. This book is the record of that discovery, a present life awakened, an old life coming back in newness, revised and re-seen and full of an unexpected grace. And leading to this affirmation (or, perhaps, hypothesis):

Stupendous beauty and power surround us. Are us.
Whosoever will become open to them will be changed.

St. Eustache

It appears I've come to Paris in order to go to church.

It's a strange choice. Here I am in the world capital of culture, intellect, the chic of smartness. I'm living and working in an artist's and writer's residency: the Cité des arts international. All around me are those four hundred museums that Parisians like to mention. I try to tally them: museums for any taste, any period; museums of armor and weapons, hunting rifles and stuffed game, gizmos and technology; New Guinean fetishes, eroticism, medicine, Freemasonry; Balzac, Chopin, Picasso, in fact painters and writers without end; grandiose museums like Musée du l'Homme (anthropology) or museums that specialize in obsessions (locks and keys, smoking, playing cards, the thirties). New art is exhibited continually—big Palais, little Palais, Tokyo Palais. Of course, there is canonical painting and sculpture over at the Louvre and a feast of nineteenth-century kitsch across the river at the Musée D'Orsay, housed under its coffered nineteenth-century railway dome. And, within the tubed frightfulness of the Pompidou, all those seething moderns. There is cinema everywhere and photography shows big and little and edgy gallery-like little collections (Maison Rouge!) . . . and the insurmountable list of historic buildings, churches, parks.

And so much more. Isn't all that the reason a guy like me comes to Paris?

There's also the Paris of indulgence. Of shopping, which I simply refuse. Of food, if you can afford it. And of sex, ditto. Didn't people used to come to Paris to have "a naughty weekend," as Auden said? It must still be around here somewhere. But no . . .

Somehow I have managed to find the Puritan's version of the naughty weekend. Here I am, sneaking off to church.

⇐

To speak plainly, I come for the organ. A particular organ, in a particular church. That was, and is, the great motive. It's what gives me pleasure. And

pleasure is really what's behind everything, high art or base pursuit. So all
this church-going, I might ask myself—is it fun? Well, not exactly. Satisfy-
ing?: yes. That's what I have to explain.

How to get at it?

The lostness, off and on, for much of my life, despite massive good luck
and frequent happiness. There was an emptiness and ways of filling it that
were not always sordid. No, not always. But under the strange furor of living,
and under the lostness, always there was something deeper yet. Something
delicious. And possible.

I felt it. It could not be spoken.

Whose story doesn't start in lostness, and perhaps end there too, in
the emptied corpse? Pride, vanity, futility. It's a lot of what we share, after
all. Emptiness in its different forms has been tearing up the world for a long
time. It is doing so now, accelerating even as we breathe and read and speak,
our emptiness at work unmaking the air, burning up the globe, prying apart
the ecosystems. Yet on we go, as if unable to imagine any change. We are that
null, that empty.

Yet something there was that said: the last word of this tale is not
vanity.

⥱

So here I am, every Sunday of my four months in Paris, walking the mile and
a half up the rue Rivoli with scarf pulled snug, passing Pascal on his tower,
turning up past night clubs on rue des Ducs, edging by the touristy square
of the Pompidou Museum—quiet at this season—then crossing before the
desolate seventies mall of Les Halles (a market ruined by too much money!)
and approaching at last the stumpy-turreted pile of St. Eustache. It really is
nothing much from the outside. Just big, as these old things are, pointy and
stony. One tower no one bothered to finish, the other forlorn.

I head to the side door as usual, and there is the fat woman on crutches
and the very fat man sitting on an overturned bucket, and today a small dark
sun-wizened man beside him. All hands out, as usual. As usual, I brush past,
noticing my hard-heartedness. Then I am inside removing my hat.

Entering St. Eustache is like changing your mind for another one
cooler and deeper. I feel it on my face, the backs of my hands—like coming
into a cave. Within the echoing space is a general quietness, larger.

When your eyes adjust, its structure is all length and height, columns
rising and rising until even the widest nave seems narrow, with arches far

above interlinked like tree branches in a grove. The eyes travel across to recesses mostly dark, perhaps soot-stained, then ascend again into mote-swum space, alive in light entering by round windows: east window gleaming in morning sun, north just a glow, south not yet illuminated but streaming clear soft light from a line of plain windows arched above a columned walk-way, coyly human in scale, midway up. As if someone could stroll up there, amidst the hugeness, and look back down at me admiringly. I'd like a turn.

I think this every time, like it was a smart new thought. I notice this and smile. Somehow it is permissible here to think the familiar, even the obvious. To think in a well-worn way.

Waiting for the music, there are other kinds of music. Walls like stone cliffs, vaults overhead fanned and connected, and we here below with our anty motion, our clicking heels and sudden-echoed chair-scrapes and lull of lowered voices. Over everything, the light moves delicately, clear light, colored light. A volume of space is defined, it is huge but we are not just within it, we are engaged, located.

I like to sit off to one side in the transept—the cross-bar of the cross-shaped layout. It's my habitual hedge: in the middle of things but edging toward escape. But I don't want escape. I want to be here. This is significant space, human space. And also—how to say it?—more than that. It calls and echoes from some greater humanity.

It challenges my hard-shelled individualism. For this place speaks of so many other humans. You feel their stories, five centuries of them: in the odd monuments, remains, reminders; in old languages and spellings; in painted saints next to crypts of the wealthy and well born who have paid for their pretentions. This place surely embodies not only a shared hope and sense of beauty, but also a practical toughness—how they got it built. Obviously, stories of money and politics are here too. As everywhere. And priests spouting dogma, as well as priests quietly binding up the needy and the wounded. A spectacle of virtues and vices then, vivid, human, enduring. All this you can sense. And also how, curiously, perhaps paradoxically, it draws all toward this end—this result—of lifting the spirit, inviting it.

Have I mentioned that I am no believer? Nothing of that left in me. No dead god, no resurrection, no flighty angels nor magical intervenings nor pious eyes-on-the-afterlife. None of it.

The suddenness of entering fully three-dimensional space activates my mind, though in a way that seems purely (almost merely) physical. My head rocks back and rests at a familiar angle, as when taking in a spacious grove all tilt and sway, dappled light and fretwork of branches. What I feel here is a roominess of rumination, a dome of presentness, round as a brain. I could take you to specific places at home in forested Portland where you would feel it too, out in the big woods of cedar and fir, where you would be stunned by the height, the complexity, crossed by light and movement, the whiff and murmur of other lives. But really, any well-arbored country lane will do just as well. France is full of them. Ahead, the road turning; here-between, the loose tunnel of forwardness; but above, the branches interlocking, the ramifying limes or chestnuts or oaks suddenly spreading you up and out. You are enlarged, fuller of possibility.

It is a feeling behind the forehead. It is like an extended mind, the cavern of thought blown out into shared space.

The enlargement of consciousness caused by this extreme dimensionality feels about the same to me, whether St. Eustache or Douglas-fir grove. This cannot be accidental. And I do not think it can be trivial.

Everyday life on city roads is quite two-dimensional: left-right, forward-back. It tends to focus on immediate goals, the next ten or hundred feet, the prize at the end of the maze. It is mostly about the money-life, linear, striving, and intentional. Yet perhaps in us an older primate mind craves another dimension. Craves the largeness of choice, the near-infinity of pathways. Three-dimensionality speaks of a different, more open way of going forward, branch by branch, step by step. A choosing way, all possibility.

In this kind of space at St. Eustache, I find I can sit by the hour, tilting my head back. I especially like looking at the North Transept. Over shadowy nothing-special exits, boxed in the usual way with plain plywood push-doors, an expanse of stonework rises. There's the big round window always changing its light, the way rivers do, minute by minute. And about halfway up, that triforium gallery of small, human-sized arches running right across, little pillars between them, lit from the clerestories above. And there's me up there, always the same tickle of imagination, childish, as if I were some churchwarden's little boy, allowed to run free amid the secrets and possibilities.

The place is as long as a football field and tall enough to fly in—over a hundred feet from stone floor to the crossed arches of the ceiling. At the little glassed-in welcome booth, you can get all the facts in a brochure written in English or Czech or what-have-you. It took a hundred years to build, was finished in 1637—long enough after the Renaissance that the underlying Gothic church was simplified, the arches rounded (most of them), the cornices and capitals and stone moldings squared off, linear, spare. The mixture works better than you might imagine. It leaves a clearness, a decency, restrained and soaring at the same time.

≡

So, it's off to church for me. I really can't believe it.

I am resident in Paris for an unbelievable four months—four months in what may be the heart of the world's cultural capital. I stay in a building full of the smart and the talented: painters and musicians and the like. Each of us has a live-in studio space, though in my case the studio is my partner's: I am allowed in as an *accompagnateur*. In Paris I'm as thin as glass, on no one's radar, free to read, to write, and to see.

I should be smoking Gauloises somewhere! I should be staring in that vacant knowing way that says I won't be taken in by any of it, the past, the present, the beautiful, the ugly. Least of all by the supposed sublimity of churches and organ music. I should be like Hemingway or Fitzgerald, it's ten a.m., time to get drunk! Yet off I go to church, often several times a week: to visit though not attend, to hear a choir or visiting organist, to tilt and think in my off-center way.

And certainly I enter every Sunday promptly at 10:45 a.m., when Jean Guillou makes his elegant, white-maned entrance to sit at the huge blond wood console, drawn out into the middle of the watchers, and play before the service: hands flying, feet dancing in snug polished pumps, surrounding us in the chords and arpeggios, the breathy flutes and booming diapasons emanating from fifty or a hundred feet behind and above, the vast organ pipes themselves covering the back wall, furnished forth in wood with carven statues, David right and St. Eustache himself left. The organ is the best I've ever heard, the biggest in France and surely among the finest in the world. And the sound. The sound . . .

I know this feeling. It has been my companion for nearly all of the long, found-and-lost-again walk of my life: I am under a night sky, starry; I am silent on a peak, weary, afraid, delighted; I am submerged in the wilds of music; I am ten years old, alone in the forest for the first time; or I am simply inside, far inside, the seeming limits of a poem. And the little hairs stand up on the back of the hands, the arms, the neck. The strangely welcome chill goes briefly down the back. And the head feels like it is a million miles across.

It is joyous, bewildering. Its old-fashioned name is *the sublime*. Another name for awe, but meaning what, really? A smallness in the presence of the great beyond. A respondent largeness that arises from within. A strange near-terror mixed with joy. Joy. Unaccountable joy.

A gladness to the brink of dread.

At Home (or Not) in Paris

So I lived for a winter and part of a spring in Paris. It was largely a matter of wandering on foot, of woolgathering and reading and observing the famous self-importance of this place, its curious grandeur and nonsense, its intricate mix of the bygone and the à-la-mode. The rue de Bons-Enfants, the rue de Mauvaise-Garçons—the good children and the bad boys, what more could any wanderer ask? And the Parisians, so brisk and well dressed yet so very afraid of any color but black, correct and unassailable black. And their language, so tricksy and charming to hear, so deeply beloved, so demanding. And the beautiful quietude of winter, when rain-slick squares go empty of tourists and their darting shoals of swindlers, when cold winds scour the sidewalks and late slanting light might briefly transform all the towers, domes, and noble façades, rendering golden even the endless six-story boulevards of expensive vacancy.

"The Cité," as we called it, is an artists' residency, a five-story building giving each artist or writer or musician a generous studio—*un atelier*—but just a tiny corner to live in. Two cots and a hotplate! Yet a kind of luxury, for when we raised our eyes all of Paris was shouldered and rooved around us: westward to the dome of the Pantheon, southwest to the black tower of Montparnasse and the distant summit of Montmartre. Daily we looked across the Seine past the corbels and slates of Notre Dame, which felt close enough to touch.

In an easy quarter-mile radius were seven bridges and six *boulangeries*. Each bridge offered four views: forward and back, upstream and down. Each boulangerie offered a regular baguette and, for twenty or thirty more euro-cents, a crusty *tradition* delicious with nothing but butter. Each day I chose a direction, a shop, a bread. Each day I chose one side of a bridge and stopped. Took in the light, changing in each minute, endless.

For Paris is a place to consider being human, locked in history and yet at liberty to know beauty, to be touched largely, at the core, dangerously. A painting might be the occasion. I saw a Vermeer . . . a Bosch . . . a strange squiggle of modernity. They did something to me. I saw an old building and a new one that drew me into a larger self, public, enriched. I wandered by churches made for this purpose, and some of them failed, mere piles of money and pretension. But some of course did not—despite my objections, they touched me. Other sources were oddly diminutive, inward like poetry. "Pocket sublimes" I took to calling them, with a laugh—as if you could snap up the galaxies in a pencil case and take them with you. (You can.) I heard music and made music too, Schubert so close that it hurt, Bach so large he filled everything, told everything. This was my Paris: a kind of intense presentness that led me to reconsider everything that had brought me here.

Which all sounds very glam and amazing et cetera, except that I often find it lonely: people all around me with whom I cannot really talk. In the Cité itself it's not bad. These are worldly folks and most of them are quite at home in English. And it's a big place—a hundred residents at least. But venturing out . . . passing daily by my favorite wino for instance. It takes me two months of striding by him, there on the Paris sidewalk with his cup out and his missing teeth, before I finally stop to talk.

And when I do it surprises me. I would usually rather observe people than mix it up with them. And certainly not in this French language that defeats me at least half the time, words flying indistinguishably past my ears until my quacking *Quoi? Quoi?* calls a halt. Unless I'm in a damn bright mood, I'm likely to avoid conversation, not seek it out—and certainly with misfits and winos.

Down on the corner are the other bums, boisterous, edgy. A burly blond with a barking dog and a Spanish flag parks his shopping cart every day by the crosswalk and sits there, begging and cajoling. He sounds angry. At night I hear him bellowing at the other homeless who come to sleep in the street-level arcade of our building. Some of them holler back. I hear banging, swearing, three a.m., four a.m. Our windows are just four floors up. I sleep with earplugs.

But when I come walking home in the late evening, they are tranquil. Their bodies line up in dirt-colored sleeping bags on the marble-floored loggia formed by the overhang of the building, stretched out in front of show windows of touching domesticity: picture-framer's shop; travel agency; and a long display of couches, plushy and new, before which the sleepers sprawl on pads of cardboard or pads of nothing at all, always motionless, out cold. I see a woman's long hair, disheveled, concealing. I see knit caps, hoods. Never a face. Drawn near are their pushcarts full of dark trash bags stuffed and wedged, or lashed nautically, or tied as a child ties, every which way. Some just gaping mouths and spilling debris.

They are always gone by the time my morning arrives. This is no doubt the deal: they must vanish. There's a limit to it, but you have to like the French egalitarianism that allows lost souls to sleep here overnight, out of the rain. I'm a guest too, come to think of it—enjoying this lucky turn that lets me live in Paris, *janvier* to *avril*, at the *Cité internationale des arts*. It's a big institution, stolid on the right bank, overlooking the expensive end of the Ile de St Louis and the spires of Notre Dame, on the edge of the once-edgy Marais. Never in my foreseeable life could I afford such a location. And so I am mumble-tongued yet elated, free in that unconnected way that sometimes makes for productivity. Every day I walk, I write, I walk some more.

My bum, the one I will eventually try to talk to, does not come here to sleep. Where he goes I have no idea. During the day, he sits quiet against his wall, alone, away from the shouting and derangement.

≡

I believe, theoretically, in the humanity of these people. I just don't like them very much. Everything about them violates my sense of decency, privacy, self-regard. A Victorian voice in my head wants to say to them, *Good god, man, pull yourself together!* And I don't want strangers accosting me, either, to demand money—money!—for nothing. Nothing! Who do you think you are, to speak to me thus?

My wino sits quietly on a box, exactly halfway down the block, leaning against a building. Parisians snap by in their scarves and black coats. He doesn't smell. He doesn't obstruct anyone's way. He doesn't pick a narrow place to set his cup out where passing toes might tip it, punt it, force some tangle of pity and embarrassment that could (so the scam evidently goes) result in cash. You could see it five or ten times in a twenty-minute walk around this neighborhood, everyone edging by some bum squatting across the crowded sidewalk. Though of course this dodge doesn't work on me. I am not available for manipulation. Hard as marble. It's my métier.

He raises his face, its kind eyes and dirty cheeks. He says, with gaps in the lower teeth: *Bonjour, M'sieur.* Or: *Bonsoir, M'sieur.*

So I nod at him and return, *Bonjour, bonsoir.* Over the weeks I begin to make a point of smiling, of catching his eye. You know, to humanize the contact. His response is unchanging, undemanding, just the clean white paper cup held before him. And just: *Bonjour, bonsoir.* In time I add money to the transaction. Twenty euro-cents, even fifty. Because, for me, it *is* a transaction, we're trading something. Unlike the disconnected druggies and drunks who imply that I owe them. This one, he implies nothing. He just smiles. I smile back.

Here and there I do have conversations in French. I can express myself, though of course missing nuances and forgetting subjunctives and always guessing wildly about gender (*la? le?* I resort to the flat, all-purpose American *luh* that must sound so wretched to the precise French ear). Still, I can ask for whatever I need, and once in a while I dare a volley of small talk with a clerk or an elevator passenger. Two sentences along, however, out quacks the *Quoi?* And communication reverts to gestures and pointing.

My Paris life falls strangely mute. Some days—most days, to speak the truth—it's easier to pass among the crowds without a word. I'm an outsider, reticent and wary. A few weeks of this, a month, and I feel my own sense of competence strangely shaken. I have to push myself to try again. And again.

For example, mumbling and bumbling my way into the Piscine Berlioux—a vast indoor pool right in the middle of town. I've had a good week sending essays back to the States, and so, feeling confident but a little buttery, I seek out the exercise. Yes, there I am, violating the clean floors of the changing room with my street shoes (I have overlooked the sign, big as day: *Pas de Chausseurs*), then needing help to figure out the coin-op locker from a tiny Asian woman in a striped smock, who gestures and points and who speaks French with, I think, both a heavy accent and a lisp. Nevertheless, I mostly understand her. A moment of success! Really, it's hard to express how this feels—the minute by minute linguistic disasters, the small, intense victories, the infinitesimal sense of human connection. She goes back to pushing a mop around the men in bare feet, who retreat to little booths to strip. I walk barefoot toward the pool. I have looked up the vocab. I am ready.

The French are a Cartesian people, rule-oriented and orderly (when not wrangling, which they also love). Right away, the pool presents tricky questions. Which lane to swim in? Each is dedicated both to a stroke—*bress, libre, papillon*—and a speed. I pick *libre,* freestyle, and, uh, *moyen,* medium speed. But am I, really? I'm a terrible swimmer, though stubborn enough to go for thirty or forty-five minutes. Buff guys in my lane speed past me, bumping my hands, my feet. I flail on. Flailing gives a very good cardio workout, by the way.

But at the end of a single lap, an official taps my head. I bob up, pull off my goggles, try to hear. *Quoi? Quoi?* French. Then hand gestures: swim-cap required for hair (what hair? I might reasonably ask). And no boxer-cut suit. Speedos. I am sent back dripping into the changing room, and there is the Asian lady, ready to help. She shows me the vending machine, but it wants twenty-five euros. For a ridiculous suitlet I'd rather not wear! I look shocked. "*C'est très cher!*" I exclaim. Ah, she nods, she smiles. And takes me by the arm to her utility room, where there is an extra suit, left behind by someone, hanging from a peg. She gives me to understand that it's washed, clean. And that there's a cap. I too smile, nod.

And yes, there I am, in the sort of tight, tiny suit I never imagined wearing in public, all six foot something of my gaunt frame, pale skin, bits and pieces. There to swim correctly, I think, with no further misadventures. Except that, when it is time to return the rinsed and wrung-out suit, I have no change for a tip, nothing but big bills. So I just smile and nod, *merci, bonsoir*. But I'm dissatisfied with myself all the long cool walk back home. I love those euro coins, those ones and twos so solid in the hand. Would have been perfect. Something for something, even up.

=

That was the same week, I think, that I finally talked to the bum. I saw him down the block and remembered the right word: homeless, unsheltered, *sans-abri*, which has a good sound. Sans-abri. Of course I know we don't say wino or bum any more. Sometimes I do it for effect, or for clarity, some sort of lunge toward plain speaking. Against jargon. It was a wintery late afternoon, clear light already plunging down into blue darkness, and a ghost moon floating above. Parisians hurrying by. Bridges, lights, moon afloat— like a dream of Paris, a painting, surreal and glowing. I caught his eye, I had a euro and gave it. And I asked his name—thinking I'd start with that, nothing fancy. Just trade names.

"No français!" he said. "Bulgarie! No français." He shrugged, shrunk back on his perch.

I was surprised. In fact I had been gearing myself up as I approached, forming more French phrases I might use. Some of them came out fast.

"How are you called? *Je m'appelle David.*" I touched my breast, gestured toward him. "*David. Et vous?*"

"Bulgarie! No français," he repeated, looking up at me helplessly. "Bonjour, bonsoir, merci. No français."

I shrugged back. Smiled as kindly as I could. There in the cup was the euro coin, the measure, I guess, of our connection. I waved and walked home.

=

I think of it often, in these months since. Is it a puzzle for me to solve? Is there someone I should talk to, something I should do? He's still out there, his kind eyes, his missing teeth. I drop coins. I smile, nod. It's Paris, but the mobs aren't here yet. Just us, temporaries and permanents, snapping by on errands and trysts, or sitting vacantly, or sauntering toward coffee on musing walks.

It is like we are trying to carry too much in our hands and everything spills out into plain view, encumbering the sidewalk; and then we are needing help, getting it, nodding, smiling. Glad to get away. But we cannot, quite, get away. There is something between people, even strangers—something shared, oceanic, immeasurable. It embarrasses us, since the forms of connection are meager.

For there is, equally, that silence. Always that. A person—any person not yourself, bum or beloved—is a lunar remoteness, tugging we know not how, meaning we know not what.

And yet we do know. But what then?

The Flatness [memnoir]

I had returned, after college and grad school, to live for a time in various other parts of Los Angeles. I endured more than a decade, seeking to teach, finding bad jobs in obscure places that might be far inland, lost in the flatness under the unyielding sun of noon or one o'clock or three o'clock, the smog-grit accumulating under my collar, the featureless, pointless vistas of glinting parking lots and low mean buildings. I knew it too well, from having grown up here.

Somewhere on the horizon might be blue mountains. I'd go there when I could, up and up into clear air and forest shade and a brief sense that all was not yet lost. But for most of this life all that was just shimmering memory.

LA is an easy target, and these complaints are almost rituals, the self-important kabuki of a certain kind of person. But I was hoping for something else, needing something rich and strange. Willing to struggle to find it. All I can say is that I feared the flatness. It made me feel low and mean myself, meagre, sightless in the glare.

===

So I begin here: desert heat. Already hinting, building, an early hour, was it seven o'clock? Six? Jags of the hot day already drifting, surprising against the almost-brisk *coolth* (we called it that, to make a joke) that still lay thick along the ground—pooled, I could almost see it, so tangible the pleasure, the skinfeel, the ease of it as I relaxed into long strides, long breathing, arms low-swung beside the hips, hands loose, shoulders free as if oiled and gimballed. Under my running shoes the dust itself had reserved the merciful overnight damp, and it sent a kind of spacious cavern presence into the nose, a cool wet stony smell that made me feel I would be able to run forever. Forever.

Ah god, the lightness, the freedom. The earnest uselessness of it. Yet like a treasure to recall—if I don't think too clearly about it. Remembering is only fun if you do it that way.

Eventually a straightaway, unshadowed and fully cloaked with the cooked air of the basin, would dispel the illusion. I'd done this sort of thing too often to doubt it. In time my core would start heating up, I'd have to slacken the pace and all would become grit and gut.

For now, though, the soothe of early morning. I had nine miles in mind, at a nice pace of maybe six and a half minutes a mile that I knew I could sustain almost indefinitely, canny to conserve, to ride free and "stay within yourself" as we used to say. It meant not to get wild-limbed, not to overstride or fall into breathing deficit, just to stay on form and in sync. To let the whole thing run, the body, all its defects and ugliness, its cable and meat and bone: a single thing, integrated (for now), glad to work, be working, be running.

Off to my right stretched a dish-flat expanse of strip malls, corner malls, overbroad roadways, parking. A place called . . . let's call it Haven, for laughs. Haven of cock-tease California views, snowy ranges wavering through the risen heat of asphalt. Haven of treeless seemingly deserted mobile home subdivisions. Haven of rock landscaping, front, back, and sides, volcanic rubble tipped from a dump truck in chocolate brown, stony gray, or an implausible green (as if to say: *See? See? And I never have to cut it!*). Haven of the gray and the bald, tipped from Midwest snow-states, becoming visible evenings at five o'clock on their after-dinner constitutionals in Kmart Burberrys—though it would still be ninety degrees—bundled up, liver-spotted, full of race jokes and complaints about music/kids/prices, glimmering button eyes or cloudy ones that didn't really track. Plaid pants up to here, wigs. In the Denny's parking lot at 4:30 in the afternoon (*dinnertime*) their spotless boxy ten-year-old Fords and Chryslers bore Reagan stickers. They couldn't wait for November to vote him in. He represented them. He was their best self. What they didn't know, he didn't know (*we made sure of that*, as he said). I see it a little clearer now: he made the whole country Haven. The whole world. No wonder they love him still.

Me, I went for runs. Burned off my angers, my fears. Kept to myself, judged people, readied my escape. I had intellect, relative youth—surely there was a better job somewhere for a PhD, why not me? (Three years already on the meter, no decent publications, when would I really take hold?)

Since the uphill was mild, the hour still early, I pushed to get a good clean burn. I was on something like a country road that wound among hills of sagebrush and baked rock. One of those old guys had told me about it a year ago, standing in line in a hardware store where I couldn't escape his chat. It proved to be a good road, though. Sometimes in the notch where one hill met another would be a dry creek, some cottonwoods. That was heaven, brief. But there I would downshift, push hard through the transition, power into the next climb. This meant: *never slack off, ever.* What I thought would win me a life. What I thought would work.

When I reached the upper flats I dipped my head, shook out my arms, loosened again into the steady pace I called *coyote* that I could do for hours. Far ahead, still invisible, would be a lone spruce or fir I had once used as a turnaround point. Past it, I believed, the road would loop and connect back to a dirt-road intersection that was now miles behind me. It felt good to have a goal, to surpass myself. It's what I had. What would work.

Running-wise, all was right. No particular aches, just an odd noisy breathing that had appeared in my right ear. An ear tube had opened up and made a gasping-chamber, distracting, unpleasant. I'd had it before. Something about exertion. Made it hard to hear.

But I held form, let the ear-noise be what it was, zenned past it. Just another obstacle, another hill, hot day, whatever. I had nine miles in mind, a certain pace, a landmark ahead. On the map it looked good. Would the little summit with its green tree give me a confirming view, the road curling back as I thought? Too soon to worry. I knew how to relax, how to float, how to never give up. I seldom failed when I had a thing in mind. Of course, this tactic had not so far answered the hanging question of what exactly I was to do with my life. I supposed this meant simply: *try harder.*

So this is the picture: Just past the boundary of thirty years, clad in baggy nylon trunks and my thinnest T-shirt, the one that let the air through, with a red bandanna folded and tied around my long poorly barbered hair, wire-rim glasses tucked in snug, and Tiger running shoes beneath me. I was miles out and approaching unknown territory. Legs good, breathing good, arms good, hearing going to pieces. No one in sight, anywhere, just sad lean me, my two yards of bone and flank.

Came the fir or spruce, sole on its hillside. Came the next turn, the new trail. The view. This part, at least, right. Exactly right.

—

A half mile ahead was a building. Even this far away it looked big, with nothing around it except a paved road coming up from the far side and two pickups parked at random angles. No one in sight.

Barn? Warehouse? I relaxed the pace, glided, allowed myself to look around. I could see it was a tilt-up building, yes. It seemed as long as a

football field. Really, it did—I can see it still. A vast rectangle, green cor-
rugated siding, peaked roof, no eaves. Just a windowless acre of panels bolted
together, hard-edged, already catching sun and sending up heat-shimmer
amid the weeds.

No one stirred. No rancher, farmer, worker. Just this *thing* in the landscape. I jogged closer, my gaspy breathing quieter, sweat drying on my neck.
It got bigger. More out of scale. The up-breeze hot.

Disconnected, like a thing that had landed from somewhere. Really,
your mind goes a strange way when you're just pounding along. It was just
so bright and so still.

And then, the sound. Suddenly it reached me. It came as if from
nowhere or from everywhere: a thousand little croaks or creaks or calls. A
shimmer of noise, a disturbing sheen rising like sunstrike from the enormous
tin structure. It was two stories high at least, shaped like a child's drawing of
a house but broad as a factory, with tall double doors and an empty loading
dock. And it was crying out in the morning light.

I stopped short of its shadow. The noise was everywhere, a cloak of
sound, inescapable, bad ear, good ear. I wiped my forehead with a shirttail,
wished for water. Stopping was bad juju: the invented necessity of a run, you
couldn't afford to mess with it. But this nowhere, this sonic weirdness, this
thousand-voiced despair . . .

Then it came to me: chickens. This was where eggs came from. Or
drumsticks and thighs. These were their voices, trapped in an echoing
shed—surely air-conditioned? But that sound, awful and wrong, penetrat-
ing, inescapable. I thought of Dante, which I'd taught once to undergraduates though I'd never formally studied it. *Voices like leaves in a dust-devil
whirlwind.* Something like that.

I felt heat on my shoulders. I pushed off. Left the chicken-hell behind
me. Took the turn leading back. Tried to feel happy about the prospect of
meeting my goal.

≡

This should be a good story. It should mean something, right? The running
nowhere. The gasping in my ear. The Poultry Inferno with its audible despair. It was the worst sound I had ever heard. I hear it now. Decades have
passed, and I still don't know what it means. It did not awaken me from
my torpor. It did not offer answers, or make me kinder. I did not become a
writer. Not then, anyway.

What did happen: I got bullied, maybe shoved, certainly almost beaten up by a guy who was, in absolute terms, double my size. I can see him now, as through sweat-fogged glasses, a face-balloon of beefy red rage floating above me. Later I learned that he was a former NFL lineman. This should have been obvious. But apparently, braininess aside, I do not necessarily notice the obvious: a smaller man waving, waving in the road far ahead; words being shouted. What was I thinking? I might have had Dante in mind, something profound or profound-adjacent. I could be absent-minded that way. It is certain that I was not hearing exactly right.

That was it, truthfully: the hearing problem. I was two or three miles past the chickens. I'd gotten into a good fast pace (the one I called *hawk*), loose and fast on the very edge of my capacity, inspired by the slight downgrade and the leafy ranches along one side of the road. I was flying. Then, way down there in front of me, in the middle of the road, by a fenced corral and a barn nestled into cottonwoods: that guy shouting and waving. As I got closer, I slowed of course but kept going. What could I do but keep going? That was all I had. Or else I could stop, a displaced geek in nylon, skinny and gasping. The heroism of a long fearless run, how instantly it becomes pathetic.

Did he yell, "Stop!"? Who knows. I heard nothing but my own breathing, in and out, rasping and noisy.

The waving guy kept mouthing something I still couldn't hear, but now I had arrived so finally I slowed to a walk. Hands on hips in that tired-runner way, hangdog. You've seen it; it means *nothing much left*. Sweat dripping off my face.

In the corral, something bad was happening. A brown colt with white marks on its face and long delicate-looking limbs was flailing, leaping. Spooked, he sprinted into a wild hairpin turn, then flung himself against the fencing. I was just ten feet away, and I saw the top plank splinter. The colt rebounded and raced the other way. I thought there was blood, and then the giant man appeared in the corral trying to stop him or catch him—windmilling, stumbling, useless, it must have been years since he was fast enough for this—so he wheeled around and stormed through a gate, bellowing and enraged. Right at me.

Out in the road, I suddenly saw his helper, a saddle-broke teenager. He knew what was coming, and he wanted to help me. The bellowing man approached, and I stood there stupidly, stock-still as I always am when I should be fighting or getting away. The boy came close and said, *Just go. Don't answer him. He gets this way . . . Just go on.* The boy's face showed worry for me. In hindsight, this is touching. It may have reached me even then. That he—or anyone—should care for me! It was a natural impulse, of course, but that didn't make it any less kindly. So I started to walk on. The colt bounded again, someone else shouted, and the enormous man was upon me.

The boy maneuvered between us as if by accident, not really looking up at the big man. The boy was saying, *He couldn't hear . . . couldn't hear me . . .* So, like a dope, I stopped and turned. Perhaps I thought that if there was talking, I would do okay. It's my other skill, besides never giving up. I can talk; I know many words.

But in this case, I didn't actually say much. For one thing I was still pulling in deep breaths, panting. And for another, the man had the thickest neck imaginable; he was four feet across at the shoulders it seemed, bald on top, and buzz cut. His cheek fat blended with neck fat. In the middle of it all was a red button nose and a gaping mouth with yellow teeth and tobacco stink. He was not hearing whatever I managed to say. It is possible that what I said made the situation worse.

Did he really shove me? I can see it in my mind, feel the handprints on my chest. But that must have been some other day, some other stupidity. Because if he had, I'd surely have awakened in a hospital, or at a minimum picked myself up from a gravel shoulder, bleeding. That did not happen. Probably the boy saved me. I know that he kept swiveling and looking bash-fully down at the man's feet, while keeping up a soothing rain of words: *He couldn't hear, he couldn't hear, just let him go.*

So I went. I walked and when the barn had blocked view of the colt and corral and broken fence, I began to jog. When I glanced back the big man was still standing there, shoulders heaving with anger, looking from me to the corral and then back again. I saw the boy over by the gate, holding it, waiting for his boss, or dad, or whoever he was to come through. From their body language I understood that the colt had stopped his flinging and now just needed care.

I could say: I have skirted various hells. I could say: I wanted to be wor-thy. I could say: I have been underdressed and poorly defended for most of my life, though a kind of paradoxical manliness has arisen from me anyway, something enduring, inept, fey, well intentioned, and lost. I could say that I have, miraculously, avoided unnecessary roughness. Usually. Not by skill, not by planning. More by . . . what? Luck. And occasional kindness. Yes: Despite my deafness, my obtuseness, my flawed theory of how to make my life into something beautiful and effective, kindness has made the difference more often than anything else. Though it would be years before I started to think about that.

I went to those hills to try to win something back from the flatness, to make the day better, the week better, to force it toward some kind of verticality. Despite everything. Now I think that whatever the sublime means, it must be an answer to this flatness. Answer incomplete. Impossible to own or even understand. But answer nonetheless.

The NFL guy ran a ranch for delinquent boys, bad boys of the sort I had always avoided. Even in high school, even in junior high, when they sat in the back, and I sat in the front. I was the sort who talked to grownups; in fact, I preferred it, while the bad boys traded coarse jokes and grunted one-liners from behind. Same thing in college, where I liked my profs and wondered at the incomprehension and flirting that filled the room behind me. Other people seemed to be making their lives of something else altogether, while I sought to understand, put words to things, find a pattern of what was good and true and enduring and unshakable, that would make me strong and thus—so I believed—save me.

Schubert: It Is a Question

It is a question.

What does it mean, this last piano sonata Schubert wrote in his short, round life? Why have I brought it in this strange loop: shipped from a German publisher all the way to Portland, then returned in my baggage to Europe? The music itself is strange, meandering—as full of byways and interludes as a forest walk. It blithely leaves one key for another and then another. Measure by measure the ground shifts, the light changes, minor, major, drifting away and coming back. For Schubert is quicksilver: never a regret, never a hesitation. Nothing surprises him: Let it come, he says, let it come.

Let what come, exactly? Perhaps that is the question.

I have been playing the *Sonata in B-flat Major* for nearly a year. Or, if not playing it, playing *in* it. I am not noticeably gifted. All my life I have listened to far more music than I've played, or could play, and in fact, I've been savoring a recording of this very piece, interpreted by the renowned Alfred Brendel, for years. The sonata shares the CD with Schubert's more famous piece, "The Wanderer," and for a while I confused the two. In my abstracted way, I hummed themes from the one and the other promiscuously.

And then one day I listened anew. I had recently begun playing the piano much more for some reason, revisiting my old Chopin and pressing forward on a Mozart sonata (six months of work) and one moderately difficult three-voiced Bach (a full year to fluency, if not mastery). And one day, listening, the Schubert came to me privately, urgently. Something in it stirred me, made me glad, melancholy, thoughtful. Rejoicing. Everything that music can do, all the illusory heavens.

But could I play it? That was my opening question, unanswerable at the time. So in a music shop, long before leaving for Paris, surrounded by pianos, guitars, drums, and fat cheat-books, I ordered the music from a bored young clerk, who I assumed must be a far better musician than I. I thought, bravely: I'll noodle in the parts I like to hear, just to see, to feel. That was the start.

But why, suddenly, the daily practice after so many years of indiscipline? Perhaps *that* is the question.

≡

I have long treasured the sonata's opening, all *moderato* in friendly and understated chords, quite playable. But before the bottom of the page, it moves into rippling left-hand arpeggios (runs) while the right hand plays a simple song. *I can do this*, I discovered, surprised and perhaps a little self satisfied. I explored forward: the next page not so bad. And on the next came a figure my hands loved to make. Thus was I launched.

My "Urtext" edition, bound in light cardboard covers of gray-blue from the Munich publisher G. Henle Verlag, comprises thirty-three pages in four sections. The first movement is generous and changeable; the last is fast and flashy (I wonder if I'll even attempt it). I have entered the sonata gingerly, persistently. It is laughable, I know: even after months, I am still working my way through the long first movement. And all the while, I admit, I have been sneaking forward into the middle movements, like stealing apples from a neighbor's grove: learning the brief Scherzo, bright and twinkly as such things are, and coming to rest in the beloved Andante, the slow movement whose nestled center is all honeyed light and amber chords, bracketed by bookends of rocking lullaby boat-song.

Meanwhile, onward in the first. County by county, lane by lane, measure by measure I walk, or stumble, asking my questions.

What are you, really?

Can I play?

≡

But for weeks now in Paris I've been laboring on the same nineteen measures. It's January, and I wish to settle in. For too long I've been fudging these measures, fumbling past and promising to come back some day to work them out properly. But they are the lynchpin of the first-movement journey, and now, with rain and wet in the windows and the stone city all around me, *now* is the time. I imagine that a "real pianist" would have dispatched them in a few days, but for me they are a bramble patch. Everything catches; my fingers can't get through.

Several times a week, for most of an hour or sometimes more, I sit down to these nineteen measures. Their story at first seems obvious. Schubert has steered the first six pages through mercurial changes, coming at last to a half-page of treble sweetness. But then three ostentatiously minor chords intrude. It is a conventional moment, even a bit clichéd: the chords announce the "minor development," where melodies are reheard in a different mood, somber, chastened, the third tone lowered like voices at bedside.

A minor development like this can go on indefinitely, can turn tragic. But Shubert offers only the briefest of darkenings, a mere summer rain shower. Somehow, by the foot of the page, darkness is forgotten in a sunny A-chord arpeggio, a simple down-and-up figure in the right, with a chord in the left. Nothing could be easier, storm clouds gone. And the next two bars play a lyric that ripples and glints—a moment that has always charmed me. But I need a full week to get it into my hands: two bars of four beats each! Lord, the repetition. The clumsiness. My limitations shock and disappoint. Yet day after day I return. Sometimes I use the Rule of Thirteen: practice a thing this many times and it will become habit. (Double and redouble, as necessary.) I make tally marks on a sticky note, notching my determination.

And yes, in time it comes. The clearness, I can hear it now under my fingers and in the air around me; sometimes I go right through without thinking, without consideration or fear or self-accusation. It is like light, like youth, like I was a better person.

≡

Oh but this is a long story. On a particular day I have mastered merely the first four of those nineteen difficult measures—I call them the Nineteen Labors. After another skipping A-scale, a single measure confronts me like an impassable boulder. It is a diminished chord broken into bits, sharps and flats scattered across the measure, fragmentary, decentered. They are called "accidentals" because they're not in the expected key, asking the finger to travel a half-tone into thin air, away from known sense and predictability. Worse, that weird x-like symbol intrudes, a thing my eye never reads cor-rectly at first, that says raise the accident *two* half steps. And anyway, what key is a diminished chord? No key, all keys, it's like dropping a drawer full of silverware.

Can I play this? The answer today is: no.

Next day I slow down, analyze. I come to understand why these pieces and bits have been flung here. I see that diminished chords resolve into other chords: they're like doorways, they go places. Magic doorways with com-plicated locks. But my fingers refuse to remember the combinations; they cannot take it all in. I am dead stopped.

I will come back tomorrow. And the day after. We'll see.

―

I have reason to forgive myself. The *Sonata in B-flat Major* seems playable to me—theoretically—but I have seen it bring a trained master to grief.

This was in Rome, a half year ago, where we had stopped en route to other destinations. The stage was simply set: a piano placed amid the ruins of an ancient temple, the Theater of Marcellus, beside an intact wall and arching loggia that made a suitable sound-shell for the performance. Our chairs were arrayed in intimate semicircles, and the concert was to start once night had fallen. Soon the drama of lighting and darkness began to heighten our sense of this place. Above us, the white hill-topping gloriousities of *Il Vittoriano*. Close by, four ancient columns, illuminated, towering. And before us, the long gleaming piano, its lid shut against the evening air, to be raised when the performer arrived.

I won't name him. But from the program's Italian I gleaned his credentials: conservatory degree, impressive performances and venues, and—yes!—a set of Schubert recordings. I often seek out music while travelling, but this concert had become a priority when I saw its second half devoted to "my" Schubert sonata. I would learn from him, I told myself, internalize his rhythms, feel the emotional beats, grasp the inner logic. All in the balmy night of Rome, with lighted monuments in all directions!

The performer appeared, a dark-haired man of middle stature and middle years. His opening pair of Mozart sonatas glided by. Intermission came and went, and the moment arrived: those opening chords, that moderate and calm *andante* tempo, the walking pace I so love—sober and reflective yet moving and moving, never stopping.

The heartbeat-tempo of life, I always think.

This prosperous calm was soon followed by those softly surging left-hand arpeggios. They need to be understated, muted: like running water half-heard under a conversation, with the clear bell tones of the right hand laid over them. But right away there was trouble. The pianist's left hand got louder as the passage unfolded, then faster and still louder, until finally crashing into the next passage, which is complicated but still asking for calmness . . . asking but not receiving. The pianist barged through that section, too, again playing faster and faster, louder and louder, until at the end he was just stabbing his hand at the keyboard, desperately, as if trying to make it stop.

Well, it did stop. Eventually. One section paused before the next. I looked at my partner. *What is happening?* our eyebrows wondered.

The sonata continued in some forlorn space between tragedy and farce. The slow parts went okay. But as soon as technical passages intervened, hurry and anxiety seemed to overtake the player, getting worse and worse until again he was just clubbing away with his hands—take *that* and *that* and *that!* At one point he gave up and jumped to the next section. I knew it. Certainly, we all felt it. But what was the right response? Pity for him? Or pity for ourselves? For we were all caught in a performance of obscure degradation.

In the Nineteen Labors, he slaved away. In the amber heart, he failed to listen. In the fast sections he panicked. Exactly like I do, whenever people are staring, hearing, noticing. Exactly my panic. I've had it since I was ten: a sense that my imperfection was shameful and revealing. That music was a test to be passed (or failed)—not a gift to be shared.

The Roman evening came down damply on our shoulders. Somehow we got through the rest of the Schubert, pondering the struggle of this pianist. Clearly something awful lay in the background, some trauma that had destroyed his poise and buried his talent under an avalanche of fear, until—despite his credentials!—he had been reduced to these tourist concerts, displaying his incapacity nightly like a weird penance. He was a ruin, himself. But it was not illuminating to see him.

Except in this sense: It awakened a sense of forgiveness: for him and thus, in fairness, for myself. It reframed the question of my own playing, so lacking in gift or promise. *If he can fail, maybe it's okay for me to fail, sometimes, also.*

A dawning recognition came as well, that a seldom-discussed dimension of music is *risk*: how it is performed in public without a safety net; how it asks for a steely discipline that nevertheless floats, glides aloft with concentrated dreamlike ease . . . always with the chance to fall, painfully, unmistakably, publically.

How it calls for grace, in other words.

Paris brings it all back. I am thinking hard about this, playing in my allotted hours, seeing, listening.

One day we go to one of the oldest churches in town, and probably the tiniest: Sainte-Julien-le-Pauvre. It is a low, sloping little button of stone that seems like it might have been at the bottom of a river for a while, so worn and smooth is it. If you've been to Paris and walked from Notre Dame over the bridge to the Left Bank, perhaps to stop at Shakespeare and Company for a dose of English-language literature, you've glanced at it just across a small memorial park. It, too, is the scene of piano concerts.

Once again I am eager, this time for an all-Chopin concert. In the city of Chopin! Where I have stood at the Chopin grave! (And found it *alive*, all days and all seasons, with boughs and flowers and tokens of love left by people from anywhere in the world. Such is the evergreen life of music.)

A tiny old church. Again the magnificent piano. Again the wait, the appearance, the applause. And the music.

Chopin is difficult. It flourishes like some celestial fluid, coursing and shining. It is insanely demanding, a known brilliance in the concert repertory. And this pianist: Oh, no fear, he never stumbled. No, he proved to be that poor Roman performer's anti-particle, his Bizarro twin. There was no fear at all. No hesitation. In fact, no music. What there was, was speed.

Feverish technical speed. And nothing else.

It was as if he would best Brendel and Horowitz and the memory of Chopin himself by arriving at the finish line first. By having more technique than anyone else. By playing faster. By *winning*.

So fast and over-fast it was almost funny. Almost. But we left with ears bruised and hearts oddly leaden, unsure whether we had been hoaxed or mugged.

⸺

Between winning and losing there has to be something else. But what is it?

I posed this question often in the following days, walking the city, hearing and seeing, thinking and humming. And I asked it in the silent moments before settling in to my little *salon de répétition* with its upright piano, where I practiced during my months at the Cité, alone yet so often fearing who might be overhearing. The same fear that has hobbled me all my life, believing on some wordless level that my unworthiness and meagerness would be exposed once and for all in my playing—that the broken, mistake-riddled sounds I made would prove everything. Everything.

Such thinking makes a frozen sort of musician. The natural thing is for music to find ears, *n'est-ce pas?* But I could play decently, satisfyingly, only when alone. Completely alone. How was I to leave off this soliloquizing, playing like the last man on Earth, as if into the void? Only much later did the answer come to me.

Balthasar Denner, Bill Viola: The Grace of Humans

My encounter with her began simply enough: a plain face, forthrightly painted.

It was in the aftermath of my long-anticipated return to the Louvre's two Vermeers. Stunned by their ability to call me again and again by their light, their precision, I had at length released myself from the paintings and sought out the Rembrandt rooms for contrast. After that I simply walked, tired of the exaltation, the strain of solemnity. How many rooms did I pace, seeing but not seeing?

And here was her middle-aged face in the plain light of day, neither emerging from darkness nor gilded with inexpressible meaning. A modest painting, you would say, neither large nor small and nothing fancy in composition either. Its background is null, a gray-black anywhere. From it the woman gazes out at a three-quarterish angle, head and shoulders filling the portrait space. A handsome woman yet far from pretty or glamourous. She has bumps and lines, just like the rest of us.

The only ceremony the portrait offers is a sky-blue snood or scarf drawn loosely across her head and down around her neck, framing a suggestion of reserve and dignity. It is an eloquent color, of course; virgins have appeared in blue for a thousand years. But this is a sensible face, grounded in time, worldly and, I think, compassionate. I gaze at it and realize that I want this face for a friend, a sister, even a mother. She is not old . . . yet. But softness around the mouth and eyes shows ripening, a vigor becoming autumnal.

The German painter Balthasar Denner produced this portrait, known simply as *Woman with a Blue Hood* during his stay in London between 1721 and 1728. He had known early success. At the age of twenty-four he was painting miniatures of German dukes and their family members and within a few years he had developed his signature style: portrait heads of women (and later, men) whose advancing years are presented in a spirit of calm

celebration. Truthful to wrinkles and sags, their faces are nonetheless engaged, alive. In fact, the first of these paintings won him wealth and acclaim
when Emperor Charles VI purchased it for the astronomical sum of 4,700
guilders. Denner never again wanted for patrons and wellborn customers.
But the path he followed, the subject and style—it surprises. The painting
the emperor bought was intended as a show of technique, and in careerist
terms it certainly succeeded. But something more happened, as it so often
does. One starts playing around with an étude, an essay, a trial, a try. And
then . . .

Say you are a painter. The days of Michelangelo and Caravaggio are
distant, done. Rembrandt, too: his era of exotically lavish commercialism is
over. Even Poussin is past, the dead smoothness of moralizing pomp. You ask
yourself: what is left when Romans and Israelites and saints have been painted
to exhaustion? Denner's is the century of Enlightenment. And his painting is
what comes after the orgy of darkness and drama and grandeur. The plainness
speaks to me. I look again at the Blue-Hooded Woman, and I imagine her as
a friend of Newton or Leibnitz, a confidant of Encyclopedists, a leavening
presence in a salon of preening Philosophs. I think she is capable of anything,
but she will not tell you what. No triumph escapes her expression, no vanity.

She is, perhaps, the person I have wished to be: unsurprised by the
world's perfidy and pettiness, unshaken by it, and yet never losing the ability
to see past it, to catch glimpses of beauty and kindness. Even of truth.

I look closer and discover that she is painted on copper—as are, it turns
out, many of the best of Denner's portraits. Some kind of light is contained
(and released) in this medium. It is an inner light, you could say. The aged
and the middle-aged whom Denner paints are people marked by the dust
and heat of life. In them we see the long road but also, mysteriously visible,
the possibility of simple dignity and honesty.

It is the faith of the classics, as old as a Greek statue or a Stoic philosopher. To spend time with the classical is to consider a life of virtue,
self-control, wisdom, and balance. It is to be far from the revels and terrors
of the Dionysian, that dark dreamscape of the raw and the wild. Too far, I
sometimes think, yet how drawn I am to this poise! How I love its reminder
that we can be, even in our failing flesh, truthful and brave.

I feel the need of this reassurance. I'm not young myself, and the sharp
edge of cynicism comes too easily to me. And just lately, another challenge:
my aged parents, who reached their nineties remarkably whole and handsome, have fallen at last into mortal weakness. Father suddenly reft of his

memory, adrift in an unmoored present. And Mother, a person mostly of privilege and leisure, suddenly expected to make decisions and stand resolute where, in fifty years, I've never known her to do so.

They are much on my mind, this winter in Paris—an odd tug, a retrograde motion. I have been a good son but in name only. I show up, and I am correct in my behavior. But their beliefs and fears have long sealed them off from me; I am the gay son they never wanted, though they have always loved me as far as they were able—a sincere, hobbled kind of love. We do not speak of it. Or of anything, really. And I have never (but once) challenged these restraints. After that I retreated into the obligatory politeness.

=

As I walk along the rue Rivoli a couple of weeks later, images of Denner and the bewildering spectacle of my aging parents are still on my mind. My long residency in Paris gives luxuries of time and place I could never afford in my life as a teacher. I'll write another book, I think, though I have given up believing I'll ever sell very many. It is oddly freeing to be so obscure. So I stroll and linger, consider what to cook in our tiny kitchen, divide my days between looking and thinking and stringing words together. It is strange to be casting back to my parents in such a place and time: this Paris winter.

Today I am heading for the Bill Viola exhibition at the Grand Palais. It is a huge show, monumental like Viola's work itself. I know what to expect, for ten years ago I caught his mid-career retrospective at San Francisco MoMA. In formats often as wide as a room or as tall as a small building, Viola's ultra-slow-motion video projections transformed the stillness of painting and portraiture into an almost imperceptible blooming; his human subjects lit, suspended, vast, and profoundly revealing.

The new show is well attended, like everything good in Paris. How brisk and seeking are these urbane French! They line up on sidewalks and pack the halls everywhere in town all winter long: painting *expos* and film festivals and photographic shows. Insatiable Parisians, eager and laughing and disputing.

And yet, as I watch in these darkened rooms, even sophisticates are changed by the classicism of Viola. The work is simple, direct: studies of single figures or small groups, set against whatever is elemental: fire, water, gravity, life, death. Gigantic projected figures rise, or fall, or disappear with a mythic silence, an achingly slow inevitability. In the carpeted chambers we fall into a hush. People pad in, stand for a minute, fifteen minutes, half an hour . . . while the opposite of exciting unfolds frame by frame, and we cannot take our eyes off it. Really, when has any show of art commanded such patience from its audience? We stand. We lean. We sit with backs against soft-felted walls. All is darkness, except whatever light the projection spreads across us. This watching is like waiting. And we wait like yogis, like mothers, like newborns.

One room in particular: a screen fifteen feet wide shows five adults in a tight grouping, almost a huddle. They are lit without drama, dressed in everyday clothes. Their eyes are fixed on something unfolding directly ahead of them, over our heads or perhaps right in our midst. They stare straight ahead, they watch, they witness. In time you see that their postures and expressions are changing. A middle-aged man's hand rises, rises, finally touching in unconscious tenderness the shoulder of the woman just to his left. The woman's face is caught in an emotion I read as resolute and resisting. Her strong, exposed arms are crossed fiercely in front of her breast and, pushing hard against fear and revelation, she does not notice the hand of the gentleman. He in turn is shocked but bows his head before the inevitable, accepts it. In this agonizing slow motion, his yielding is monumental, awful—like Job before the whirlwind.

They are in a shared reality yet each version is distinct. In front of them a younger man, perhaps thirty, seems stricken: his face is all pain, all loss. His mouth gapes open, crying out soundlessly. This grief is hard to watch.

Resistance, acceptance, brokenness. It is a species of sublime that Viola brings us to, both beautiful and threatening. That these moments can be shared, yet be so utterly personal and private—this is in itself a sort of miracle.

They are five humans of differing ages, four men and one woman. The title is *The Quintet of the Astonished*. Over its fifteen minutes of barely moving stillness the projection spans a range of human emotions wider and deeper than anything I have ever seen represented except, perhaps, in the best productions of Hamlet or Lear, the deepest of Sophocles. Perhaps certain operas. And those all take hours.

It is the eldest of the quintet who, for me, carries the event into transcendence. Centered in the back tier, he seems at first to welcome the astonishment: he basks in it, absorbs it, his lined face open as a sunflower. But moment by moment he moves toward some deeper space, until at the end his head has tilted back, eyes have closed ecstatically, and one hand spreads wide like a star below his face. Enraptured, confirmed, translated.

What has he seen? Something you've been hoping to see, all these years. Something pointed toward in scriptures, vedas, sutras. Something the great Teachers have conveyed only in koans, parables, hints, and gestures. You have glimpsed it perhaps in hospitals or seen it flicker by on city streets, fleeting. After all these years, you still wonder what it is. You still hope and doubt at the same time.

After a long time, a strange time somehow off the clock, I sighed and looked around me. So many faces in the reflected light. Each one so still, so unguarded, so moved. And suddenly I saw that Viola had filled the room with people made patient and strong and accepting: we had become Iphigenias and Horatios, Dorothea Brookses and Tom Joads. Viola's five people on the screen had become fifty, or a hundred, in the room—a rolling silent wave entering and finally leaving the darkness, each of us illuminated, each moved toward utterly private depths that were yet completely shared. This was, simply, human space. But the *best* of human space, where we found our better selves.

And then I am outside, returned to Paris, where I walk, an almost mute stranger, seeing those around me with new and wondering eyes.

⸗

A few weeks later, I decide to return to the Blue-Hooded Woman. Somewhere on the way, threading through the Dutch and Flemish rooms, I come across a gray-haired painter working at imitation. She has set up her easel before a pious bit of old-mastery, a varnished saint in a northern landscape. Visitors come and go, but she regards only the painting, trying to catch its light, its color. With a little shock I suddenly imagine my own mother: the small, neat, gray person, brisk and keen. Exactly. My troubling mother took up painting in her sixties, and she showed remarkable fluency with the brush almost immediately. In thirty years she has taken lessons, kept at it, filled rooms and hallways and storage closets with good works and bad ones too, I admit it. She is thoughtless in some ways but ever working.

I have a still life of hers at my home in far-off Oregon that I show to my friends. It's just a few flowers in oranges and reds, standing raggedly in a yellow clay pot. But it has an undeniable presence, the kind of presence she was seldom allowed in her married life, where she played the little woman, pert and childlike, always in service to the posturing husband who made all decisions, big or small. He loved her to the limit of his capacity, I believe. But such love, and such service, became burdens they feared to put down. So they never did. There developed around my mother an unseen world of trying to cope: hints of alcohol, Valium, unspoken accusations, sick headaches, and long afternoons in bed.

She works only from photos and other people's paintings, my mother. She copies the copies, and the wonder is that even so, some of them come to life. They do.

In her blue hood, Denner's woman looks out at me from an indeterminate darkness without detail. Its slight brushwork relief of gray or deep green recalls Viola's featureless backdrop. She too is brightly, clearly lit. All is seen. The rest doesn't matter.

This time I notice weariness in her eyes, despite the calm that originally attracted me. A history weighs on her. Her mouth has the resolve of someone who has *lived through*, who has endured. She is more worn than I recalled. "Yet still attractive," I was about to say . . . but that misses the truth. Her calm is earned, her character built, achieved. This is her radiance.

This is the classicism not of flawless statuary athletes and smooth-limbed maidens but of determined sages—Epictetus, Marcus Aurelius—who know that no one escapes trouble and time, and who counsel a lofty, stoic detachment. This is both the attraction and the chill behind the classical.

Denner himself did not escape trouble. At the age of eight he sustained an injury that never properly healed. Biographers don't know exactly what happened, but he limped for the rest of his life. The historian records: "His convalescence was very slow and he was forced to sit still for long periods of time. To cope with his boredom the boy sketched pictures of the people and things around him. . . ."

He was lucky in his parents. They were plain people, though rising: his father a dyer of cloth but also a well-known Mennonite minister; his mother recorded simply by her name. They saw their housebound son's talent and engaged for him a painting master in watercolors and later another in oils. At sixteen, young Balthasar was placed in an uncle's business and given clerical work, something sedentary and suited—so they must have thought—for the lamed boy. But on his own time he practiced and painted, fierce, gifted. By the age of twenty, he was ready to be launched. The rest was brilliance: patronage, renown, and soon marriage and a happy family.

Denner was sixty when death began to strike, sudden and overwhelming. First his mother, then his beautiful and talented daughter Catharina, who bore her mother's name. She had been the family's music, playing the violin or piano for long portrait sittings, for family celebrations, for the sheer joy of it. She must have left a very deep and aching silence. Soon Denner's father went too. For a year and more, Denner painted nothing. Nothing, after a lifetime of nearly unceasing industry.

The darkness behind a portrait—it is real.

Yet a portrait is never just a story about its creator. Or its sitter. Something else happens, a creative alchemy that frees it from the lurking double biography. And it is this freedom that gazes out at me here, from this unknown woman in blue, captured in her humanity: that we may be enmeshed in our circumstance—trammeled, caught—and yet be ourselves.

Denner eventually returned to his studio. He lived a few more years, left forty-six unfinished paintings. His tale is no melodrama. Just a normal life, in happiness and talent exceptional, though shaped by pain and grief. Shaped but not distorted.

This is what I take from the classicism of Denner and Viola: a robust humanism that refuses to elevate darkness above light. A humanism that regards the pains and losses we all suffer with a realistic equanimity, trusting that we can rise—will rise—to stand and say a calm, hard-earned, and even tear-stained *yes*.

This is a shared *yes*, despite the solitude of our individual lives. And it is the best task of the artist to remind us of our great, imperfect togetherness in this journey. In my bones I feel it, this assertion hundreds of years in its arrival or delivered from a contemporary. It is a more sober response to the great terrors, the dark destroying passages of life. Nothing histrionic, no tympani roll of stage grandeur. Just this: the answer given by dignity. The sublimity of acceptance.

Coda

My mother has astonished me. The evasive woman I have known since I entered my teens—the person whose pretensions and feigned incapacities I could predict with lasered precision—has stepped into the new challenge of caring for my father with an unprecedented calm. She speaks to me without disguise for the first time in my adult life. And I, also for the first time, find myself in actual conversation with her. She is lonely for her spouse, now half disappeared. She admits it: *This is hard*, she says. She weeps, briefly, on my chest. Then she straightens her ninety-one-year-old shoulders: *No more of that*, she says, dashing the tears with the back of a hand. And marches off to set out his dinner and see him safely seated.

Perhaps she was, all along, the mother I thought I wanted. The mystery—the darkness—has been this: how hard it has been for us to actually see each other.

Schlock and Awe [memnoir]

It is a cooling-off Sunday evening in August. Billy Graham is preaching, way down from where I sit on the infield. He stands on a wooden dais: just him, a pulpit, a microphone, and a big Bible, which he holds floppy in his left hand while his right hand goes up into the air, pointing, or chops down decisively, thrillingly. What he points to, that's what we want to point to. What he chops, that's what we chop.

He says that America is in a moral crisis that could destroy us. Something about race. And definitely about sex. A greater danger, he says, than the Russians. Or even the mighty Communist Chinese in their millions. I am listening very intently.

The seating seems to pour down the sides of the Los Angeles Coliseum. It is steep, dizzying. I've never been in such a big space. Every seat is filled. The playing field, too, is filled with people on folding chairs, placed on a white tarp, canvas I guess. We've been told this is the largest single meeting ever, the biggest . . . in LA history? Crusade history? Human history? There are tens of thousands of us and thousands more outside the stadium who could not get in, hearing it on loudspeakers.

Billy Graham is preaching. He tells us that in all the galaxy with its millions of stars, we are the only part of God's creation that is lost. Lost! In all that loneliness of space, only us. Us.

Me.

⇒

Before the preaching began, a silver-haired gentleman with an impressive three-layer name sang to us: George. Beverly. Shea. His song was big too: "How Great Thou Art." When he sang it, a current of feeling passed right around the gigantic oval—a shared feeling such as I had never experienced. His voice was a rich, sustaining baritone; it flooded the whole stadium with God's power and vastness:

I see the stars,
I hear the rolllllling thunder...

Behind him the choir sang, filling the skies. I got goose bumps, tears. Five thousand voices! Standing in the curve of the Coliseum behind the platform, rising up row after row in the various robes of their own church choirs, but all united, astonishing, huge.

So when Reverend Graham himself finally took the stage, and the audience stirred and applauded and leaned forward—it was as if we were all one. A big, big feeling.

Billy Graham is preaching. The mike makes him intimate like a best friend, and he warms us up slowly. His voice is close and sincere, until suddenly he is shouting and his words echo from the loudspeakers right across and back again. You can measure the space by it, and it is filled. And we are filled. Exalted.

Everything he says is what I already believe. But he makes me certain. I'm as sure as I could be of anything. The emotions prove it. The thousands. The millions.

I am thirteen, ready to do business for Jesus.

⸺

The feeling that went through us, it was so convincing. So deeply desired. A combination of fear and pleasure. A sense of our own smallness and the greatness of God, whom we could, maybe, somehow, become part of. We were and were not within the scale of Him.

It was a kind of kitchy, Christ-y Nuremburg, wasn't it? Orchestrated, arranged for effect, staged. I see that now, as I look back.

That is the problem with the sublime: It can be mustered at will, made the ventriloquist puppet for whoever has the means. It can be made to speak for God. For the Blessed Virgin. For Country. It can speak for The Reich or The Soviet or The People's Republic. It can speak for The Corporation. The People. Capitalism. Communism. New Thought. Est. America.

And it works.

⸺

I am thirteen, and I am ready to do business for Jesus. But there are obstacles.

It has only been a few months since I walked into the baptismal pool at the front of our church, wearing a white zip-up that covered me to my wrists and ankles. Pastor Travaille, a pleasant man with nice hair, getting burly with middle age, had been waiting in the water, beckoning me to come from a side door and walk down the four or five steps into the pool. He put a hand on my shoulder and had me face the congregation. Just as he had done with the others, he asked if I believed sincerely, if I had accepted Jesus as my Personal Lord and Savior. I needed to find my voice to answer, but I did: YES. Then he held a folded white hanky over my nose and mouth and placed his left hand with a surprising tenderness under the back of my head and laid me backward into the water until I was submerged.

At other baptisms I had noticed that it was never quite smooth after that: the coming-up part was always splashy; people wobbled and struggled to their feet. And when they walked out the other side door, their white onesie was sure to be drippy and clingy, and of course their hair would be plastered down over their eyes.

But this is not my problem.

⚌

A man called Cliff Barrows is leading the choir. Billy Graham is saying, in his soft southern accent, very intensely: "I'm going to ask *hundreds* of you to raise your hand, right now, if you wish a closer walk with Jesus. Right now. *Thousands* of you. I am going to ask you to come forward now. Now. Just as you are. Come forward now. *Hundreds* of you are moving toward the aisles, *thousands* of you. Just stand up and walk to the aisle. Come down to the railing where your brothers and sisters in Christ are waiting to help you . . ."

And the choir, five thousand strong, sings softly. Earlier it had lifted us like angelic legions. But now "Just as I Am" floats out so quietly, yet filling the night air! I have tears in my eyes, but I am not moving. I am nailed to my seat. Terrified, alone, sinful. I cannot go.

⚌

The baptism service had been held just for the three of us. We had known each other for years in Sunday School, and now we had turned thirteen, which meant the Age of Accountability. Pastor said: time to take your

decision for Christ and make it public. We took classes to learn about the
Bible and understand what we were supposed to believe. Now it was early
summer, a Sunday evening service.

When we had all been through the pool, we were to change out of the
wet garments in the back room next to the pastor's study. We stood on green
linoleum tile. There was nubbly yellow church glass in the windows, and it
was dusk, but the twilight was still glowing through.

Tommy took off his onesie, and, like all of us, had wet white shorts on
under it. Paul took off his onesie. I did too. We made a little pile of them,
and water pooled on the green linoleum and reflected the yellow light in the
dimness of the back room. No one had thought to turn on the lights yet; it
was that sort of in-between hour.

Tommy had muscles already. I looked at him, on the other side of the
softly shining wet floor. He looked . . . amazing. I was taller but bean-pole
thin. Hopeless.

Our undershorts were sopping so we took them off too. Paul was still
a little boy. I wasn't. And Tommy . . .

Tommy in the reflected light. The nubbly golden light playing up his
legs. His torso, with its unmistakable definition of muscles. His chest. His
shoulders. Perfectly shaped, handsome, potent. Tommy.

Oh my god.

=

If I came forward at the Coliseum, I would have to talk to someone from our
church. It was all organized. You went down the steep sloping aisle toward
the field. You waited your turn, since really a lot of people were coming
down, pouring down, all together under the singing and the coaxing voice
of Billy. Then a Helper asked what church you were from, and a Counselor
would come from your church to talk you through it.

This had all been explained to us on the bus coming over from La
Crescenta First Baptist.

But I was already Saved, so that wasn't it. What was I to say? What
could I possibly say? My manly household, brothers, father, the cousin-
boys. Competing always, posturing and winning and losing. Our uncle,
who had been in show business, had a mocking little routine: he minced
and wetted a pinky finger to smooth his eyebrow and everyone laughed. I
couldn't be a fag. And I wasn't one! I never, ever minced, and I tried hard

to win, and sometimes did. Though I knew, clearly, that I was in some kind of unspeakable trouble.

I said nothing. I stayed in my seat while hundreds Came Forward. It was like drowning. Silent, motionless among all the singing people.

⸻

A few years later, when Richard Nixon was running for president, Billy Graham would call him "God's Man of the Hour." Nixon would defend Capitalism and Christianity from the Communists, Billy said. He stood beside the flag and said Nixon was the one.

That's what everyone said at church. They supported him entirely.

I shook Richard Nixon's hand in 1968, while he was running for his first term. It was a big, meaty hand, probably swollen from so many handshakes. He wasn't impressive in person: a medium-sized guy with uncertain eyes and narrow shoulders. And a nervous smile.

He was elected with a "Secret Plan" to end the war. He said if he revealed it, it wouldn't work. I was eighteen, and I wanted to vote for him. Four years later, he ran again. Same platform. Same flag. Same war. And he won, again. By then, old enough to actually vote and facing my own possible conscription, I saw right through it. I gathered myself to make a break with family, church, the lot.

The problem with the sublime is that it can be faked and often is. Any king with a golden carriage and a bejeweled crown can wow the rubes. A president has a motorcade and jets booming overhead. A priest stands beside him and anoints him on behalf of God. Anoints the whole nation, why not? Then it will be God's Nation. And everyone will feel that swoosh of emotion.

It works. That's the problem.

⸻

The fake sublime works, but only for a while. Then the air goes out of it and disillusion follows. War hysteria, then coffins. Nixon's backlash came quickly too. Without a new crisis, new enemy, new Armageddon at hand, the manufactured sublime has a short shelf life.

But the real sublime might last forever.

I never got any closer to Tommy than that one carnal, golden moment. Yet its resonance is still with me. I still wonder what it really means. Not just the easy comedy of adolescence or the canned drama of coming out. And not just the cynic's laughter at earnestness and belief.

I looked across a void and saw the power and beauty of another person. It touched me, immeasurable, unreadable. And I was never untouched again.

Though I would be solitary, even monk-like, for years.

Mount St. Sublime

Some days I think I am immune to Paris. Everywhere I see the hand of wealth and power, overscaled and underfelt. Everywhere the *hauteur*, the *glamour*. In my mind I Frenchify the word: *gla-MOUR* like Dorothy La-MOUR. Yes: Paris the vamping sexpot of cities.

Everywhere the self-declarations of greatness. The Roman triumphal arch, borrowed, imitated, admired. The broad famous avenues, where consumerism (at present) fixates upon—of all things—handbags. *Handbags!* The Mansard miles of well-appointed flats standing null and uninhabited, vacant possessions of the world's super-rich who rarely bother to visit. Even the act of eating is inflated into a religio-fiscal ritual. Oh, clothing, motorcades, fame, above all money, *money money*. It is folly, a collective delusion. The French are the best in the world at this fawning pretension. Universally admired for it. Though some days I can see that it is the cheapest of magics.

The tomb of Napoleon catches me on one of those days. How hard it tries to deify the little psychopath! How many tons of green and off-off-red marble for the obese casket on its squat, curving little legs? With a Brobdingnagian finial. It's like a piece of furniture gone mad. Set in its recess, under its dome, all of us looking down upon it with manufactured rue and groundless sorrow. *Alas, still dead after all these years!* Is not the world still glad to be rid of him? No, not if you allow this place to work its faux magic. You may descend into the crypt like Orpheus weeping into the underworld, there to see the murals that sing of famous victories. Nobody bleeds here; no one's life or family or arms or legs are shattered. Just: *La gloire.* Le gla-MOUR.

I might just be dyspeptic. Or I might be, indeed, immune to this disease.

Even the Louvre! (Much as I love its collection ... or *parts* of it, anyway.) In its excess, its bureaucratic ornament-encrusted too-muchness, it seems like a vast U-shaped turd left behind the ghastly corpulence of one Louis or another. The scale of it measures neither taste nor imagination but only grasping privilege and the prancing sycophancy that feeds it and wipes up after it—the politic of courtiers beauty spots pumps with ribbons intrigue betrayal ambition failure vanity, vanity, stinking excrescence of vanity.

Everywhere the will to impress.

Everywhere the longing for vastness.

Everywhere settling for bigness.

⇒

To walk off this mood of cynical disdain, I get myself over to the highest point in the city. Number one Métro to number twelve and off at Abbesses, then up the hilly cobbled streets and invigorating stairways of Montmartre. But though walking is, for me, a nearly infallible cure for megrims and depressions of all sorts, today I walk under a cloud. A kind of grouchy dread.

For at the top, of course, is the Basilique du Sacré-Coeur. I catch glimpses: domes numerous, pointed, and decorative. How many million tourist snapshots? Uncountable. It's the sort of thing our Victorian, sorry, Third Republic forebears loved: a gleaming white pastiche of insincerity and historical pretending. It's medieval Byzantine, as reimagined in 1875—right about when Mad King Ludwig was constructing his own medieval fantasy in Bavaria. In other words, about as real as Sleeping Beauty's Castle at Disneyland (I'm an LA boy, I know what I'm talking about here).

The French government financed the basilique in what is known as the "National Vow," a set of murky religious promises, penances, and bargains with the Divine. In the midst of losing the Franco–Prussian war (1870), the "spiritual" community of Paris floated the notion of vowing to build God a symbolic church "if we obtain . . . deliverance." Paris was spared occupation, but battlefield defeat led to the brief outbreak of the radical socialist Paris Commune (March 18 to May 28, 1871). The well-churched and well-heeled saw this as an offence to God and further evidence of national impiety. Therefore, once order was restored in the form of a wealth-friendly government, the vow was redeemed by building Sacré-Coeur exactly in the *quartier* whence the commune sprang. (The current religious purveyors of the place, of course, energetically dispute these interpretations.)

Bargaining with God has a long tradition. It surely presents an interesting kind of religiosity, assuming as it does that the creator of the cosmos *needs* whatever it is one is promising and thus can be haggled with. To speak without irony: offering the deity a quid pro quo is a staggering affront. My long-time rule of thumb: seeking to manipulate the spiritual world is superstition not spirituality (which, if anything, seeks to accept Mystery, not control it).

On the wee mount of Montmartre the turreted concoction preens and poses. All Paris looks up to it, this beacon of bathos—the spiritual equivalent of a pratfall, surely the opposite of sublime. Hiking here does not help me, despite the blessing of mild exertion. Halfway up, gazing out at the city, I pause for reflection.

＝

Once I slept at the bottom of a mountain in the lee of a lucky ridge, where trees had survived the volcanic blast of a few years earlier. At first light I arose in the company of others, quiet in the gray dawn, to do what we had come to do: hike to the top, trudge the sand and scree up, up among dodgy fresh-cooled boulders teetering on makeshift angle-of-repose gravels where gravity waited patiently to continue them on their descents. A wild place, seething, ragged. Not in the least picturesque.

It awakened little in the way of poetry or insight. Just: hike now. One leg after the other. It was our day's work. Five thousand feet of altitude to gain. For what? I wondered, gazing around at the burned-over and broken place. For what? I'd been on mountains before; this was uglier. I'd been high before; this was lower. I'd done hard climbs; this would be easier. It would achieve no great thinning of the air. Mount St. Helens was just a little eight-thousand-footer now, a stump left over from an episode of explosion.

For what? I wondered. If you tilted your head back for a second, ascending, the top looked like no top, just a wide flatness with sky above it. Nothing special: just, apparently, an end to trudging.

But then came the last three steps. Head clearing the rim. Body catching up. Eyes catapulting a mile and more across the space left by explosion, the emptiness. Before me, the void. And a full mile down, the caldera. Steamy wisps of vents and fumaroles from blocky bulges of new-cooled magma.

I stood on a horseshoe-shaped rim, a curve of truly amazing proportions circling what was left of the mountain, that once-shapely cone now blown apart and emptied. And this sudden vista internalized in me the volume of space and matter, the actual quantity of mountain that was vaporized one day. Boom. The geological forces became a sudden visceral feeling: a giddy expansion in the head, an exploding apprehension of power beyond scale. No snowy summit, no handsome peak I was ever on delivered this sense of terrible awe with such force and immediacy.

It was a moment that is called by the name sublime. This word, this feeling, that has fallen so far out of fashion, then come back to us stranger and more fashionable than ever.

Fashionable or not, I find that I cannot live without it. I find, in fact, that I have never lived without it, as far back as I can remember. When I reconstruct my life, there it is. Always there, bigger than life, deeper than thought, wider than oceans.

⇐

As a young Wordsworthian in my twenties, I read Friedrich Schiller's *On the Sublime*. Of course I was instantly smitten. Schiller laid out a clear program for the beyondness of our world and thus of ourselves. There was such lonely grandeur in the prospect from which he gazed! His words illuminated my own rather disconnected striving, cut off from others and, indeed, from myself, alienated from my faith and not yet able to affirm what would replace it. He spoke the nearly inexpressible burden of awe and ecstasy I had known in mountains and on shores, beneath night skies and in great swaying groves. He gave it warrant and dignity.

Now that I am writing about it, revisiting old texts (by the grace of the internet, even from the austerity of our atelier at the Cité!), I feel how Schiller's ideas shaped me or perhaps confirmed my path, since I had already been on it for so long. It is a solemn pleasure to read him again, to feel in retrospect the grand struggle to acknowledge the wild excess of the world and to know that this struggle was not a wrong turning but a movement of wholeness and, in fact, humility. The sublime offered a counterweight to intellect and academia, a rebuke to the vainglory of young energy. There was a fitting silence in it: a way to stand, mute and moved in the starry-sky power of infinitessimability. Made small, I grew.

Schiller (writing in the 1790s) deploys what was by then a familiar, if paradoxical, formulation. In the presence of the vastness of the natural world, a powerful "mixed feeling" arises: "a composition of melancholy which at its utmost is manifested in a shudder, and of joyousness which can mount to rapture." We experience "the sensuously infinite" of the sublime "fearlessly and with a terrible delight."

In these phrases Schiller offers his version of a deep and long-running eighteenth-century engagement with the cosmic World quite at odds with that century's rather prim neoclassical reputation. As early as the 1720s, the poet James Thomson (of "Elegy in a Country Churchyard" fame) had sounded the note in his *Seasons*, which found "Nature pressing on the heart" with "A sacred terror, a severe delight" or, elsewhere, "a pleasing dread." Emotional oxymorons like this, mugwumps of opposite feelings, soon became the keynote for all discussions of the sublime.

Along with the paradoxical language, Schiller adopted the two-part framework of his great forebear, the Irishman Edmund Burke, who had reshaped the aesthetic world with his 1757 book, *A Philosophical Enquiry into the Origin of Our Ideas of the Sublime and the Beautiful*. Burke formally introduced and codified "the sublime" as an aesthetic. His tidy taxonomy— sublime versus beautiful—seems to have been accepted without much resistance, perhaps because the sublime attracted such attention that the merely beautiful seemed uninteresting by comparison. Schiller was typical in accepting this scheme. (Immanuel Kant adopted it also, in the *Critique of Pure Reason*.)

Burke had declared that "[T]he sublime . . . always dwells on great objects, and terrible." But assuming the viewer is not in actual danger, the brush with vastness produces "not pleasure, but a sort of delightful horror, a sort of tranquility tinged with terror." One might weary of the strange litter of two-headed emotional terms: delightful horror, etc. But the verbal formula persists because, I think, it reflects the irreducible duality of our experience. We find ourselves small in the universe yet shockingly large in our feeling and intellect; we are at the same time one and many, lonely and crowded, selfish and self-sacrificing, spirit (whatever that might mean) and flesh. Burke's book went through new printings continuously for the next thirty years and still resonates today.

≡

How to understand the strange shivering compounds of delight and terror thus awakened?

Fate in the tragic perspective becomes *fatality* in the sublime. When caught in the whirlwind, the distinction seems moot. But afterward (should one survive), or viewed from a safe distance, the whirlwind of the sublime shapes a distinctly different aesthetic. The almost literally inconceivable cavalcade of reality is somehow met by a satisfaction: that the breadth of creation, after all, includes us. And includes us, *responding*. The respondent soul is measured, and it too is vast.

Thus the sublime pushes moral questions into the background, in the face of a nature for which "ought" is suddenly irrelevant. Perhaps this was part of Schiller's power for me, for I was making the selfsame transit from a moralistic fundamentalism out into an infinitely larger world, a world where the essential question was not sin but sheer existence. For me, this was a good trade.

At the end of his much-revised essay, Schiller took a turn that carried him far beyond the by-then familiar pageant of Burke's sublime. Just before publication (in 1801) he added a section considering a yet darker and more disturbing face of the sublime: the apparent "confusion" of nature, its "chaos" and "anarchy." We feel him to be our contemporary in preferring, for instance, "the spiritual disorder of a natural landscape" over "the spiritless regularity of a French garden." Schiller discovers that even the "bizarre savagery" and "wild incoherence" of nature carry a sublimity. The encounter with incomprehensibility, with morally lawless reality, delivers a fearful sense of a radical and utter freedom.

Here is a muscular aesthetic indeed. He writes:

> Let us stand face to face with the evil fatality. Not in ignorance
> of the dangers which lurk about us—for finally there must be
> an end to ignorance—only in *acquaintance* with them lies our
> salvation . . . the terrifying and magnificent spectacle.

Schiller thus opens the dangerous door that so many twentieth-century artists would walk through, grappling with the world's inexpressibility and incoherence that produces its own bewildering kind of sublimity. For most of us civilians—those without an art-school taste for the assault of incomprehensibility—this is difficult terrain. What might be called the "incoherent sublime" makes more instinctive sense encountered in a landscape, or a moonscape, than on a canvas. But I'm learning to go there. If vastness is the outer limit of the sublime, perhaps this disturbing incomprehensibility is its inner horizon. A strangeness that repels and yet seems familiar.

It was moonscape indeed on Mount St. Helens. The gaping caldera and its power-charged blowout on the north side had their effect. I quailed; I expanded; at the last, I rested lightheaded in nearly thoughtless beatitude.

But on the return slog, descending through clinkers and devastation, the ecstasy darkened. Perhaps this was just fatigue. Or perhaps it was, as Schiller had hinted, the unnerving attraction of meaningless destruction. By the time I was taking off my boots and stowing my gear in someone's car, I hardly knew what I felt. It was a confusion, rocky and disheveled.

I'm descending still, wondering when I'll get to the bottom of it.

≡

No doubt it is the Paris of the Pompidou that would respond to this mood—
a museum full of modernists bludgeoning the senses. I'll get to that in time,
for I've been having my moments there too.

But today, on Montmartre, it's just me standing outside this Sacré-
Coeur confection of churchiness, attended by surprisingly few tourists, three
discouraged buskers, and no hustlers at all that I can detect. It's as peaceful
as I've ever seen it. Under this gray winter sky, even the fakey, pointy domes
look good. Sort of.

Well. People do put shrines on mountains. Hermit huts. Shinto
temples. Monasteries. Over on the Brittany coast, where I have spent a few
months teaching from time to time, there's that ultra-touristic Mont St.
Michel, a gothic marvel on a pointed island hilltop. I confess I like it. There
is something sanctifying about high places. Even here. Yes, even here.

When I get tired of mocking Paris, I let myself step through into that
other city that is coy, momentary, antique, and of the heart: the wanderer's
Paris, old and new. If the moment comes while up on Montmartre, why
resist it? Maybe, standing here on the summit of Paris, each of us is a little
shrine of sorts, a traveling two-legged lean-to of aspiration and possibility.
Of seeing. Of vision. What was it Yeats said about the perpetual virginity
of the soul?

I turn, putting behind me the absurd minarets of haggling pseudo-piety
and voilà, there is the world. Not only Paris (as if any sentence has the right
to say "only" Paris!) but all else beside. The horizon beckons, and as Gaston
Bachelard has expressed it, we are "promoted to the dignity of the admiring
being." A wind may clip in from the Atlantic, brisking the cheek. Daylight
from the nearest star may gild and reveal. Sound may rise up from the all-
around and cause wonder. In this mind Paris can't hurt you; you might as
well wander there. It is no further from the truth than anywhere else.

Bosch in the Burning World

At the joining of the Dommel and the Aa, a town was built and called Bosch after its forest. It prospered, rivaling Utrecht in the southern part of the Netherlands. In its churches there was music. In town there was money. The two rivers were combined to make a moat for protection. "Dommel" meant drowse. "Aa" spoke for itself.

At the joining of the Dommel and the Aa, a man called after his town (and thus, a man called Forest) slipped in and out of realities, painting, succeeding, marrying, worshipping. Always succeeding. Though he slipped in and out.

At the joining of drowse and ah were visions. Daydreams. Awe perhaps, also—in the way of dreams, uncanny. Bordering on nightmare, perhaps. He painted what he saw. Though what he saw was the unseen, that world where everything mattered.

In our world, nothing seemed to matter. Our world was burning, and no one noticed.

But he did.

<hr>

Hieronymus Bosch painted Earth as blissy, fruity, naked, and ostensibly sinful. He painted bizarre musical Hell. Those are the ones everybody knows. And in 1501 he painted St. Anthony looking straight at me. Stopping me in my striding, enjoying, pleasantly privileged day. Stopping me, you might say, dead.

It is a hard fate to be arrested by Bosch. His canvases are moralistic, full of *contemptus mundi*—that otherworldliness I knew and rejected as a fundamentalist by committing to *this* world, and no other.

But then, "this world" ought to be plural, *worlds*, since there's so plainly more than one: the outer world and the inner. There's the catch. And there he caught me: Bosch did. St. Anthony did.

An inwardness shines out from these busy, surfacy paintings. It is hard to explain. Much easier to get caught up in the chutes-and-ladders comedy of it, the cartoon evil and the incomprehensible vice. And, really, isn't it just adorable, all this sinning and sincerity, the pinky nudes in their apparently damnable naughtiness?

In a museum in Lisbon. Decades after dropping those struggles with saintliness and purity and self-loathing. In a small room shared by a Bosch and a Holbein and a Dürer—the chamber of wonders, I called it. Full of excitement and awe, thinking I'd call my partner over to see it, to bring his savviness to bear, his ability to see. Then thinking maybe I'd just stand there a while. Silent. Wondering.

≡

St. Anthony's face, with its look of calm unsurprisedness, comes to the viewer unmediated. His eyes lock on to yours. It's as if he stood in the room, monk robes and all, placing a hand on your shoulder. I imagine he'd smell a little of cloves or fields. The "odor of sanctity," though undoubtedly, in real life he stank. But his sanctity would be the kind that makes you *want* to be human, not sorry for it, like those skin-and-bones flesh-hating hermits. Is this really there, in those soft eyes? Or am I just finding what I want to find? In history he was a founder of the monastic movement and a renowned ascetic. Yet in a museum full of soft-fleshed Virgins and radiant Christ-babies, this Anthony is the one who engages me.

On the canvas, everything around him swirls in its own spin of appetite and strangeness. Each character utterly in its own world, as you expect with Bosch—carrying on as if no one were watching. Oh, it's a riot! In the skies fly certain large fish carrying well-dressed burghers, signifying . . . something, no doubt. The vanity of wealth? The airworthiness of fish? No one knows, though as with everything Bosch there are many scholars who make sage guesses or offer elaborate keys (astrology, alchemy, secret heresy sects). Yet the painting remains a puzzle. With the fish carriages fly other demonic critters, insect-like, carrying scythes and wrangling people-prisoners. And with them sails a kind of devil's pirate sky-ship.

On the ground, just under the saint himself gazing out from the picture's central tableau, unfold two processions, left and right. Cavalcades of folly and sin, I presume. Really you can have a lot of fun just nosing up to these and seeing the hybrid creatures of tree-parts and people-parts and animal-parts, riding on donkeys, thieving and flirting and cavorting: clerics and nuns, perhaps a statue, maybe a parody of the Bible story "Flight from Egypt," an overturned cart.

Below the processions is a bridge and a pond with dream-monster fish, people riding them or imprisoned inside them and looking out, while beside the pond is, uh, a beheaded goose? Or something vaguely stomach-shaped with a gaping esophageal maw, ridden by a creature playing a lyre, and behind him a gigantic strawberry with people sprawled under it and a nun wielding a sword sitting in a cup. There. You tell me, what's this all about, except craziness? Writing can't begin to exhaust the giddy *melée* Bosch has painted. If you look, you'll get drawn in and an hour will pass before you come back. And you still won't know what you've just seen.

The *Temptation of St. Anthony* is a triptych altarpiece, with painted wings on either side of the central canvas. On the left wing, three faithful men assist the bent and exhausted saint over a little wooden bridge. Of course, this being Bosch, under the bridge are monsters or monstrous doings. Some characters reading and scheming. A messenger bird on ice skates in some sort of uniform complete with badge. And looking up, above the faithful threesome and saint, other merrymakers and lost souls and demons.

The right wing offers a calmer moment: the saint sitting, gazing again, same face, same eyes, just looking up from reading his Bible. Around him is chaos, of course: creatures, nudes, a scary old lady, a beggar. And in the background, more flying burghers above a placid Dutch landscape, windmill and all.

All in their own worlds, hermetic, sealed off. Silent. And in the middle, the gazing saint.

⇒

There in the midst St. Anthony seems to be looking out into *our* world, his eyes speaking to us. It's almost uncanny, un-Bosch-like. I have looked at the many Bosches in the Prado, more than once. I recall nothing like this! The central tableau of the painting takes place before the courtyard of a ruined church. The saint kneels at a little wall beside a grouping of well-dressed men and ladies at a round table, who seem to perform some kind of mocking ritual (a Black Mass, according to most interpreters). A pig-faced man, robed in forest green and carrying a lute, is having his pocket picked. Two figures in exotic headdresses officiate, while a clarinet-nosed demon bird tootles behind them. A beautiful woman, sumptuous in rose-pink, crowds the kneeling saint, handing the sacred dish across him, but of course he ignores her and the others. An apostate nun receives the dish while beside her a large handsome head in a green turban reclines, torso-less, on trousered legs and booted feet. Strangely composed amid this scene of vague infamy, St. Anthony gazes out and holds up two fingers in calm and blessing.

Far out on the horizon, a city burns in dusky night, windows alight, roofs ablaze, lurid red flame so bright that despite the billowing black smoke it throws a tiny shaft of light through a gap in the collapsing church walls and across the courtyard. Catastrophe burns on the horizon, dreadful in the night. But as I said, no one is noticing. No one notices anything in these Bosches. Things just go on as they always do, people locked in their pursuits. There's something immemorial here, the unending story of lust and life. The unending visitation of suffering, ignored unless it comes nigh thee.

<hr />

I was able to lay my hands on the source Bosch would certainly have known well, the medieval best-selling book of saints called *The Golden Legend*, written about 1260 by the Genoese Italian author Jacobus de Voragine. In it Anthony is tempted by devils disguising themselves and offering him all manner of enticements, starting with sex. But always he outfaces the tempters, refusing them until at last they manifest their horrible snouts and claws in rage. "Now that I have seen you in all your ugliness, I will fear you no longer," he says.

Once Anthony was being so pestered and tweaked and tempted by devils that he called out, "How can anyone escape?" And a voice answered: "Humility." Then angels lofted him to safety through the air, demons trying in vain to block the escape. It would have been fun to see this scene painted instead, perhaps yielding some air-traffic mix-ups with the airborne fish. The moment seems made-to-order for Boschy hijinks, but the painter leaves Anthony solidly on the ground, weighted with his patient gravitas.

Linguistically, *humility* roots in *humus*. There's an earthy sensibility in Anthony that surprises. Yes, he's a desert saint, distant and austere. But the stories Jacobus tells bend toward a gentle groundedness that subverts the world-hating stringency of official saintliness. Anthony's rules for living are simple and avuncular: "Don't be too quick to move somewhere else" and "Don't worry too much about the past." He recommends, not groveling privation, but *moderation*. Simply that. You could imagine him as a pretty good counselor down at the church, someone who understood being human and would try to make you less crazy with god-fearing, not more so. Though it is true Anthony tends to see Satanic beings, often of gigantic height, somehow he does not become a scary zealot. Consider this tale, my favorite, which I'll take right out of William Granger Ryan's translation:

> An archer once saw Anthony taking his ease with his brethren and was displeased at the sight. Anthony said to him, "Put an arrow to your bow and shoot!" The archer did so, but when he was ordered to do the same thing a second and third time, he said, "If I go on doing this, my bow will break!" Anthony: "So it is with us as we do God's work. If we stretch ourselves unduly, we are quickly broken, so it is good for us to relax from our rigors from time to time."

Maybe this humanity touched the artist, too—though Bosch was clearly tempted toward severity. His canvases certainly intend an unremitting sermon against the flesh. Indeed, in the town of 's-Hertogenbosch (then and now called by its nickname "den Bosch"), he belonged to two lay brotherhoods of religious conservatism and strict piety. Yet . . . who looks into his painted world and feels moralistic rigor? What we feel is something else: curiosity, fascination, confusion, bemusement. And when Bosch paints Anthony radiating a kindly beatitude, we feel not judgment but an invitation to be *more* human, not less—though in a higher register.

Viewing a Bosch painting is entering an imbroglio, a hubbub of too much, everywhere. It reminds me of the internet. The eye darts here and there, collecting randomly and ending up oversated, binged out. But in time I begin to notice the very different registers within this free-for-all: high, low, campy, and sometimes really just unreadable. In St. Anthony himself we find a portrait of warmly believable humanity. He is in our world, realistic and fleshed-out. The goblins and devils, however, seem nightmarish but denatured, their real sting absent—more like Halloween spooks in dress-up. Somewhere several levels beneath literal believability are also figures who seem to be mere painted symbols, metaphors of vice perhaps: that strange red-draped figure in the right wing, for instance, looking like a fat one-legged tummy with a huge knife stuck into it. Too weird to imagine as anything but a transform of some moralizing point, pun, or lost folk saying.

And then there are bits of actual cartooning, which I confess my inner ten-year-old likes best, among them the ice-skating Messenger Bird in the

left wing, who always seems ominous. He works for the bad guys, I think.
He's matched in the right wing by (for me) the oddest of all: an armless man
of the same size and scale and animation. He's dwarfish and draped head
to foot in a shapeless crimson cloak, making his way just above the head of
the seated saint. His visage is middle aged, prominently nosey, with a look
of stubborn personality. He bumps along in a kind of walker with a teapot
dangling from one rail. A band around his head holds a stick. Perhaps it's
a whirligig. Perhaps it's a drinking ladle, which might allow a cooperative
customer to buy a drink from the teapot. I take to calling him Tea Caddy,
until I realize that tea had not yet come to Bosch's Europe. So what's in the
pot? Beer? Water? I imagine him getting a penny a sip from a well-disposed
traveler or a Brueghel-like crew of field laborers. I like him because he doesn't
mope, he seems full of irrefrangible selfness.

I am far from feeling in control of this spectrum of registers, this range
from visual symbol and wordplay to fun-time cartoon to achingly touchable
humanity. Probably hardest to grasp is the sprinkling of elfin, almost childlike nudes, with their barely discernable sexuality that nonetheless seems to
be leading them astray. They're fey, remote, and subversively charming (as
they are in the most famous Bosch, the *Garden of Earthly Delights*). In them
the moralizing seems most prominent and most undercut at the same time.
The easiest clever move with a Bosch painting is to notice this attraction
to everything his official sermonizing deplores. Bosch is fixated, obsessed,
mesmerized by all things fleshly. He is of the devil's party and doesn't know
it. It's why we love him and find so much life in his painting—life that does
not easily resolve to a single interpretation.

Participating (directly or indirectly) in everything we claim to con-
demn, we are stuck in self-defeat or self-delusion, obsessing over details
while the world burns. It's a checkmate that can't be escaped, except by a
move in another dimension.

In the center of the center of the sprawling canvas, above the kneeling saint
and the oblivious circus around him, unfolds a strangeness of a different
kind. I've been mentally calling its locale a cavern (plants sprout from the
heaped-up ruins), but I see now that really we are looking into the dark,
far-back interior of a crumbling church. We can see straight in.

A cross is illuminated there. Christ hangs visibly from it. In front of
the cross Christ also stands gazing out at us, hand raised in blessing. And

beside Him is a table offering the Eucharist, which is also Him, of course. A threefold involution: Christ is Christ in Christ, deep in the cave in the middle of everything. Illogical, time-bending, place to get lost (and found) in, the inmost inside of the rose—mirror-maze, labyrinth, earthly path, soul's desiring.

Here the sacrifice never stops.

What sacrifice? For me, not the doctrinal one. But rather the human one, the one we experience daily, the death of the soul, despair and meagerness eating us up. And yet here we are, enduring, waking to another day another loss another outrage; here we are, fearing the worst and yet eager for more. That gazing man-god by the cross, calm and present, mirrors (or in fact models) the face and gesture of the saint. Come here, he says, and be more human. Come out from the wealth-striving and beauty-pageantry and tittle-tattle rattle of life's empty chases. Come here, come deeper. Breathe. Partake.

To breathe here is to arise, in all simplicity, to that higher register. To be present with mystery, to allow it. To be at once grounded and exalted, emptied and filled; to be spiritual in all your mere flesh. If this is not the sublime, it certainly points toward it. In this painting, as in all the great Bosches, some kind of dialogue has been opened with our dream-selves, our fear- and hope-selves. And this understanding is offered: come to terms with emptiness. Don't think you will fill it. Be as empty as you are, so that something better might flood in.

In the evangelical college where, once upon a time, I tried (in vain) to work out my salvation, I learned the Greek word *kenosis*. It refers to Christ "emptying" himself of divinity to become mortal, a self-sacrifice truly beyond measuring. The concept has stuck with me as an alternative theory of value, reversing our culture's worship of acquisition, our more-more-more insatiability. "Less" or "enough" are not values found in consumer capitalism. Yet they are found here, in this painting.

Bosch's paintings are always about that Ecclesiastes message: the world's emptiness. *Vanity of vanities, all is vanity.* It seems to me that kenosis—self-emptying—is the answer to vanity. Is the higher register of it, you might say, transforming the existential problem of vacant, meaningless wanting into an unexpected joyous paradox: a ladder of emptiness straight into the fullness, and over-fullness, of the sublime.

—

It's not that I think art will save us. We have set our world afire, and no one knows how to stop it. Going to a museum won't help. But not going to a museum won't help either.

Oh we know enough, theoretically, to roll back some of the global ecological catastrophe. We could. But we choose not to, and *that* is what no one knows how to fix. But Bosch reminds us that the world has been burning for a long, long time. Small fires, bonfires, occasional firestorms: greed and hatred at work as usual; the pinched private smolder of mere selfishness; the raging conflagration of organized tribalism. Either way it has always been quite easy not to notice your neighbor's life burning with despair or want or suffering. We have organized ourselves around armed power and the love of money. How could we be otherwise?

And now the burning world is made literal. It has escaped from the rhetoric of agitprop and sermon and begun to rage across the actual world.

Yet I never hesitated when I flew from Portland to Paris for a long residency with my partner. According to an online calculator, our airplane flights probably emitted around 1.5 tons of carbon dioxide. That's quite a lot—about as much as a half-year of driving a typical automobile. The Carbon-Footprint Calculator website says I could "offset" the whole ton and a half if I sent twenty-eight dollars to reforestation in Kenya. But I didn't. Let me stipulate what a dedicated environmentalist I am. Have been for decades. I vote right. I contribute. I compost. I drive (when in Portland) a very efficient auto that I haven't replaced in seventeen years. But if the world had to burn a little in order for me to have my winter in Paris . . . who am I to say no? Too much righteousness is, you know, unseemly.

In fact, my Bosch-watching holiday was really a holiday-from-a-holiday, for we had fled to Lisbon to get a little sun in the midst of the cold, gray Paris winter. Airfare was cheap, we'd never been to Portugal, away we went.

And it was in Lisbon that I saw the *St. Anthony*, at the Museu Nacional de Arte Antiga. (The Louvre has only one Bosch, *The Ship of Fools*, which during my stay was always out for conservation work.) So in Lisbon I'm three deep in a regress of privilege: Paris, Portugal, and the odd luxury of fixating on an ancient painting. I never question this kind of luck. Am I to sell all and give it to the poor, take up my hair shirt, hair Levi's, hair thinking, hair not-thinking, and monk myself? Obviously not.

Yet I wouldn't object to a bit more consciousness. You know, amid the plenty.

*Soon I am a Paris wanderer again, invisible and inaudible. The natives are ac-
customed to tourists who flicker and mouth bad French and disappear. They have
better things to do: governance, fashion, money. Some days a martial parade goes
by our window, clip-clopping with horse brigades and shining helmets. Not one of
us in the five stories of the Cité des arts residency knows what the occasion is, ever.*

*I tread the rue St. Antoine, street of the saint, in the old fever-swamp called
Marais, where once no one of "quality" would go. It was for the Jews. But I wander
just a few blocks and it becomes rue de Rivoli, boulevard of palaces and highlife.
Two ends of the same road.*

*I am adrift in headlines and bad news I wish I had not read. But it is
the same as always. Some murderous god-blathering true believer has rampaged
overnight. Some political buffoon has a sudden following of millions. Some sleek
counting-house princeling has explained again why the poor must be left that way.*

*Can this be real? I ask statuary Pascal, staring down from his tower. Surely
he notices the incompatibilities, the way commerce flows from and toward the
spirit, neither understanding the other. He leans as he always does, pensive and
silent.*

*And I think of that calm look of St. Anthony, which seems to answer what-
ever outrage the news is selling today. Can this be real? I ask him—my daily
disbelief.*

Yes, *he answers,* of course. What else were you expecting?

*The lack of surprise—that's what I want. As much as I can want anything,
I want that. And with it, entrance into larger, deeper space.*

Even in this waking dream of Paris, I want that.

Voices [memnoir]

Alexanderplatz

At Wittenburg the Communists became intolerable. I felt I had to act.

Dieter our guide—our "minder" really—had arranged it all: the bus from Berlin; the tour of Martin Luther's monastery, its grounds, its strangely famous outhouse. And above all the church on whose door Luther had posted Protestantism. That's what we came to see: that door, the nail-hole, if possible! Like Catholics looking for relicts and bits of true cross, we wanted It. The real thing.

And what Dieter had arranged—that was not It. Instead he brought out a neutered minister of the state-run Lutheran Church. His words burned in me like the lies I had been telling, myself: enraging, filthy, despicable. Marxism, he explained rapidly, wasn't it really what Jesus had preached? Helping the poor, equality. "So" (smiling and nodding), "here in East Germany the Christianity, it reaches already its true expression." His voice was muttering and insincere. A fleshy face, pink and well fed.

My chance came when Dr. Hieronymous, the history professor from our college who led the tour, asked if I would say grace at lunch afterward.

It was a surprisingly long and disjointed grace—a graceless grace, I'd have to say now. I stood and thanked God for our lunch, our blessings, our bus driver. I must have rambled through any number of things: America, elections, Checkpoint Charlie, spaceflight . . . I took a breath. This part is clear. *And above all our salvation in Christ Jesus who is the Way, the Truth, and the Life.* My eyes were wide open though everyone else's were closed, all forty-five of us and our three traveling profs. Even Dieter's eyes were closed. To feign respect, I supposed. *For the Truth, especially, dear Lord, we give thanks. Because You told us that the Truth would set us free. So keep us free, Lord, from the lies of those who would silence your Word and imprison your followers behind walls and false doctrines. In Jesus's Name, amen.*

Our collegians blinked open, some looking up friendly at me, encouraging. Some smirking, but I didn't care. I might be a liar and a horrible person, but at least I knew the difference—what was Christian and what was Not.

≡

Our bus brought us back to East Berlin, to the vast paved prairie of Alexanderplatz with its lone high-rise hotel, a showplace built to impress the foreigners. But we had driven many miles through the endless gray city. We had seen its flatness, its meager shops, its empty windows, its weirdly nullified citizens standing in lines here and there when we braked at intersections.

Can it really all have been so gray? That is how I remember it. Even the sky.

I was to bunk with Jim on the fourteenth floor. He hadn't smirked, I had seen that out of the corner of my eye. We dropped our bags in the room, and by almost wordless agreement we kept our coats on and headed back outside. It was October 18, cold and gusty. But we had a frisbee, and there was a *lot* of room out there.

East German soldiers apparently did not have specific instructions about frisbee-throwing foreigners. There were guards standing every fifty yards or so, all across the square kilometer of plaza. They wore gigantic overcoats and what we thought were Russian bear hats, thick eared and woolly. We'd never seen such clothing. Our evangelical college was in Santa Barbara! So we believed they might be actual Russians. We threw anyway. When the wind went slack it was easy to sail one out there, far, far and for the other guy to track it, looking up over his shoulder, speeding up, sprinting . . . and making the catch. It was a sky-blue frisbee. The only color I saw on the entire square. In the entire city.

That felt free, running like that. Making a good catch. A good throw.

Jim was handsome and self-assured. I hoped he was noticing my performance. Then, of course, I accused myself, mentally. Silently. Bitterly. I had a well-trained voice reminding me, every minute or half-minute, what lie I had just told, what uncleanness I had just committed. The running, the trying hard—that gave me a break from this voice, brief. One breath I could take.

In time one of the guards moved over toward us. He left his rifle slung over his shoulder, but he held both black-gloved hands in front of him and waved a finger: No, no, no. It wasn't frightening or aggressive. It was more like an uncle trying to keep you out of Dutch.

As he got closer I was surprised at how sweet his face looked under the giant woolly cap. And at how much I suddenly liked him. For his friendliness, his almost-apologetic look. He was no older than we were.

≡

What was fatal, I realize now, was Jim's praise. That was what I could not defend against.

He admired my resistance to the lying pseudo-Christian pastor. That was how we saw things: that the world was full of sneaky fakes to be on guard against. After lights-out, lying in our single beds, he asked me across the darkness: "Oates, how did you *do* that?" It was the strangest thing, that admiration. I could not bear it. Though I wanted it more than anything.

It triggered the single most inexplicable event of my life.

For years I had been successfully faking my way. I had disciplined my eyes not to look, my legs not to cross in the girly way, my thoughts to self-correct and self-criticize always, immediately, insistently, so that the lies I lived, the lies I told my teammates, churchmates, parents, brothers— pretending to be straight and clean and normal—so that those lies would never go unchallenged. So that I could ask God to forgive me and change me. Change me. Change me. I could show Him the bloody shirt of my self-hatred and He would know I meant business.

But praise—that could not go unchallenged. That was the unacceptable lie.

I tried to stop it. *You don't want to know.* But he insisted.

And after a pause, a strange confused moment, I heard my voice saying what I never intended to say, unthinkable, impossible. *I'm a queer. I'm a queer. And you don't want to be in the room with me.* How did those words come out of my mouth? To this day I cannot explain it.

I thought he would leave then. Really, it was that simple in my mind. What came next was ostracism, shame. What else was possible?

Jim got up from his bed. He came and sat on my bed. I was rigid with fear, with shock, expecting the worst to start now and never end. Never.

"We could pray. We *should* pray."

I couldn't respond.

"Sit up, Oates. We'll pray, and then God will take care of it."

I did as he said. Mechanically I got out of the covers, sat beside him on the bed. In our skivvies and white T-shirts. I kept a distance: two feet.

Jim reached his hand out. He put it on my right shoulder. In friendliness. In support. The warmth of his hand. The very last thing I could have foreseen: that he would touch the queer. The leper.

It broke me.

I heard a sound forced out from my lungs. I heard it. A strangled voice that was not mine seemed to come from the pit of my stomach. I heard it, and I fell to the floor like I had been struck from heaven. Or from hell.

It was like in a Pentecostal church. But there were no demons, no spirits. Just Jim in his shorts, I in mine. On the floor, curled up.

We were both surprised, dumbfounded. Nothing more happened. In a minute he said, "Well, get back up here and let's pray. And then let's get some sleep, Dude."

⇒

We talked and prayed nearly every night of that tour, the remaining months of it. I talked; he listened. We thought that God really would change me. I spooled out my shame. It seemed to help.

When we got back to the college, we roomed together. Gradually the intimacy of all that praying and talking wore thin, and we backed it off. I experimented with being less angry, but that was going to take a while. I was still suspended, secretive, ashamed.

For the next six months I wept every day, by myself, off in corners. I had been steely and dry-eyed, strictly so, since I was thirteen and had begun to realize what I was up against. So this long pent-up crying jag must have been a sort of release. It was melodramatic and self-indulgent, my truth-voice told me. I did it anyway. While I found my way.

But Jim was easy. Funny. We had a good time, most of the time.

In April a man named Robin came to recruit for his wilderness program. He was a Christian, but he said it wasn't about preaching. He wanted to take stressed teenagers, inner-city kids and lonely kids starting to get in trouble, and show them the backcountry: climbing, backpacking, being a part of a trustworthy group.

I said yes without hesitating. To spend all summer in the Sierras and even get paid! (A little.)

Jim said he had to go back to Newport Beach. Something about his father. Anyway, he was a business major, and this didn't really pencil out.

⇒

Lucy's Foot Path

After a month of planning and training and poring over maps, at last we are here. Crossing the Kern-Kings Divide. It is realer than anything I have ever done.

Seven of us new guys, plus Robin—divided into two groups. We are discovering what the High Country is all about. In just a week, our duties will begin: a busload of teenagers will arrive and need to be taught reliability at either end of a climbing rope and acclimated to altitude, bugs and dirt. And then brought out here. Here.

≡

Looking from the head of Lucy's Foot Path: to the south, Lake South America, Mt. Ericsson, and the Diamond Plateau. I am in a U-shaped flaw, a low place in the back-curved ridge that scales up from here—both sides treeless granite, fractured and whole, thirteen thousand feet and more on the sharp-edged heights.

≡

Our group has climbed Mt. Stanford and then tried for Mt. Ericsson. We started at first light, but it was a long slog. Robin began to worry that it was getting late. So he cancelled the second climb and led us to this shortcut. LeVon is dubious, uncomplaining, comical. He's a saltwater sailor far out of his comfort zone. Bob, like me, is a distance runner, so the legwork is easy, the stress of long exertion familiar. Climbing and altitude and exposed rock—all that is new to us. But we like it.

I like it.

≡

Looking north: this gap, this talus-mouthed rubbleslide. Ridges and chutes. Beyond is that pretty lake, Reflection, where we left our packs and food hauled up in trees. Between is just darkness and downclimbing, the purple of dusk coming down, coming down. And still I am standing alone, whippy wind funneling up the chute, striking at my toes and knees and face in this barren notch. Wind carrying faint voices, calling my name, calling out "Ready!" Calling out nothing at all that I can hear. Nothing at all.

≡

How easy to let the melodrama go. That's what I am thinking, though without really thinking.

It is cold here. One by one the others have disappeared down the famous chute. I watched them slide, standing and sitting, digging into the loose scree with their boot heels, getting smaller and smaller down the long bend to the right and then out of sight. Windy wait between each. We go singly because of rockfall, stones dislodged and tumbling, picking up speed, flying on ahead. Long after they disappear, I hear the rock echoes. One by one: Robin, LeVon, Bob. Now me.

Instead of pushing off to join them, I turn once more to look behind me. A jumble of slopes, snow patches, rock and ice, as these things are when you get there. Not pretty like in photos or imagined on maps.

≡

Now the details are losing out to the darkness. Whitebark pine on the far ridge, crowded together. My eyes adjusting. A flank of Mt. Ericsson. Part of Lake South America, wide, shining. Tips and facets around the Diamond Mesa.

≡

I am light headed. Dark headed.

≡

Alone now. Not the way I am alone with other people. Lucy's is unclimbable; the guys at the bottom might as well be miles away.

≡

I return to my staring. Darkness coming.

≡

The Lake. The Mountain. The Diamond.

≡

I am quiet in my mind now.

≡

God is silent. He has no further comment.

≡

The voices are silent.

―――

All around me like truth, this silence.

―――

The lake far off, still glowing with sky-shine, and stars, or planets, beginning to show.

―――

Voices from down there again, wind-carried and, for an instant, clear. I turn at last, face north. Snug the daypack, settle the bulk of goldline rope coiled over one shoulder. Step off into the scree and gravity, not saying a word.

And that will be my life for the next five years. Ten, if you want the truth. A long muted trek, distant from other people, still virginal, still striving. But grateful for the silence. The silvery, unwavering silence.

Schubert II: Counting Time

The *Cité*, our expansive block-long building, is equipped with music practice rooms, *studios de répétition*. In fact the whole top floor, the fifth, seems to be for musicians, where there are more (and bigger) pianos out of sight from the rest of us. I'm staying on the floor below, and I hear them often: the woodshedding, the drill, the outbursts of music. I don't mind. It's a sonic richness that merges with the air, the domes and roofscapes, the winter weather glowering and gleaming. And anyway, closest overhead is a Chopinist, who is glorious to hear. Down on the basement level there's a compact auditorium and stage where the musician residents play for us weekly. I am beginning to learn their names and specialties.

Each of the residential floors has a little piano practice room, available for the asking. For a fee, of course, this being Paris. In my initial request to the formidably French personage at the front desk, I take care to present my seriousness: here is my music, the Chopin, the Schubert. On my first trial, I step tentatively into the second floor studio, close the door, get the feel.

Of course better musicians surround me, *real* musicians, but I try not to imagine them listening in the hallway, waiting for the elevator perchance, thinking, *What is this awful racket?* No, such a thought is impossible, worsens my playing audibly, drains the joy from it. My old struggle with self-consciousness—how often it has shamed me! But I am determined to play past it, somehow.

No. Day by day, remote from fear and ranking judgment, I enter another world. There are four pianos to choose from, all uprights, three of them good or even excellent. I come several times a week, scheduling two-hour blocks and sampling them all. But *le troisième* (third floor) is the best by far: a Rameau whose ringing tenor fills the studio with bell-like harmonics—dizzying, delicious.

To this piano I return again and again, until the act takes on dreamlike familiarity. I enter the small room beside the elevators. I lock the door behind me, tilt back the lid, regard the window, the light, the view, the day;

open my book bag, place the music on the rack, the mechanical pencil beside; flip on the standing lamp, adjust the stool, sit. I shuffle through the limited choices I have brought with me: a few Xeroxes and the Schubert, in its slate-blue covers. Sometimes I play a Joplin waltz to get moving. Nearly always, for decisiveness, I plunge through the Bach C-minor fugue in three voices (from *The Well-Tempered Clavier*). Then the Schubert *Sonata in B-flat Major* comes forward, and I go to work.

When was I ever so wealthy in time and disposition to afford such outlays? I wonder if I am counting my days, as Schubert must have been counting his. Counting them in melody, in surprise, in grace. While we are here, all time stops.

Of course, counting time means one thing for a bungle-fingered amateur and something quite different—vastly, stirringly different—for a Franz Schubert. Yet somehow, we are in it together, aren't we?

⸻

Schubert's short life has been dressed up in all kinds of sentimental flummery. In the glittering Imperial and musical city of Vienna, he was beloved and celebrated yet always in some kind of Beethoven-shadow. Schubert often gets assigned a kind of Camille role: dying prettily, lingeringly, tragically. So romantically single. And *oh* the music he didn't get to write! And *oh* that symphony—*unfinished!* Alas, the good die young.

Yet behind the silly stagecraft of hero worship, Franz Schubert was a strangely robust little nut, nearly uncrackable and far from "good." He was a strange attractor. People came to him, couldn't get enough of him. They offered him their homes and lodgings. They put up with his excesses and even his habit of being a no-show at his own parties. When he did show, it was marvelous. But sometimes he was too hung over from nights of drinking. Or, it seems, from boy-chasing. Other times, he simply could not stomach the dullness of the "sausage-eating" bourgeoisie that kept getting invited. In the lodgings of friends or the homes of the well-to-do, his admirers mounted regular performances called "Schubertiades." Everyone has heard of these, both in 1820s Vienna and ever since. So it was more than a bit awkward when there was no Schubert.

His friends called him Schwämmerl, Little Mushroom. It suggests his diminutive stature: round and bespectacled and slightly improbable; something nocturnal, earthy, ungovernable. Pouring drink, pouring song, pouring music that he might never hear performed, always on his own path and in his own time, eager for diversion yet unswerving.

Part of me wants to write a kind of *memnoir* for Schubert, a gentle schadenfreude for poor mushroom boy. I suspect I want him as an intimate, my own little curly-haired genius pal. But the flavor of memnoir seems to be the perverse sweetness of old pain. And Schubert won't admit of it. Because his is not a story of pain: it is a story *interrupted* by pain. And the fact that it's been told otherwise for generations is just a terrible shame.

So here, my little friend, is a better tale, truer and happier (and sadder because of it). I have read around, rummaged in the journals and tomes of musicologists, witnessed their squabbles and evasions and, in my way, pieced it together.

⸗

His birth was plain and petty-bourgeois, like mine. His mother, Elisabeth, had been "in service"—a maid—before marrying Franz Theodor Schubert, son of a prosperous Czech farmer, who moved to glittering Vienna and climbed to the respected rank of Schoolmaster in record time. Franz senior became the sort of man regarded as *self-made*. And though their household was pious and strict, it seems also to have been full of music and laughter. As well as grief, of course. Of fourteen births, just five children survived. Normal enough for those times.

Little Franz attended his papa's school and got early music lessons from an inept church organist/Kapellmeister. He played viola with his father on cello and his older brothers Ignaz and Ferdinand on violin. For them he wrote his first string quartets. Ignaz tutored him on keyboard, his father on strings. I discover with delight a report that little Franz befriended a joiner's apprentice who took him on sneaking adventures into a piano warehouse where he could play on better instruments (the sort of story I hope is true). In time the great man Antonio Salieri swept into the picture, offering him lessons at seven years old and a year later a choirboy scholarship in the Imperial Seminary. There he heard music—such music. Mozart, Haydn . . . and off he went.

If "off" means on his own path, and no one else's. After his education at the musical seminary, Franz took the teacher's exam, but failed it due to a bad mark in (what else?) religion. As a lowest-rung assistant teacher he worked dutifully if intermittently, in his father's school at age sixteen, seventeen. But then he dug in his heels: *No more teaching*. His biographer Christopher

Gibbs diplomatically reports that he was said to lack "the requisite interest and patience for this profession," a profession that Schubert's friend the poet Mayrhofer more bluntly called "time-wasting, arduous, and on the whole thankless," noting too Schubert's ever-after "aversion to music teaching."

So at nineteen he began a wandering life that seemed to suit him perfectly. He began by leaving home to live with his friend Franz von Schober, an idealistic charmer regarded by some as dangerous, supposedly a bad influence on the circle of talented young men who had gathered around him. But this kind of blame can be a whitewashing tactic, diverting attention from the stubborn unconventionality that marks Schubert himself from this point on. Schubert was not led astray. He *was* astray.

Schubert had already pushed back against his father's religiosity and against bourgeois ideas of security and success. Now, instead of security, he had friends. Such friends! Their letters, remarks, and insights were gathered, a generation later, into a remarkable compendium by Otto Erich Deutsch (whose "D" numbers also formally catalog Schubert's oeuvre). From these documents biographers learn the passionate warmth of this circle of poets, musicians, painters, strivers, and admirers—how thoroughly they loved and supported one another. Writing to his "dearest and best friends" during his first trip away from Vienna, Schubert declares simply that they are "everything" to him.

The living arrangements shifted like those of college students: six months here, eight months there. The *ménage* was frankly Bohemian. Schubert's close and observant friend Eduard Bauerenfeld called their style "communistic" (in a pre-Marx, lower-case sense) and his comments are assembled by biographer Gibbs:

> Hats, boots, neckerchiefs, even coats and certain other articles of
> clothing too, if they but chanced to fit, were common property....
> Whoever was flush at the moment paid for the other, or for
> the others.... Naturally, among the three of us [Schubert,
> Bauerenfeld, and Schwind], it was Schubert who played the part
> of a Croesus and who, off and on, was swimming in money, if he
> happened to dispose of a few songs or even of a whole cycle....
> To begin with there would be high living and entertaining, with
> money being spent right and left—then we were broke again. In
> short, we alternated between want and plenty.

"Plenty" usually meant, plenty to drink. Schwämmerl liked his pint—so much so that sometimes, in letters, the topic comes up as a troubling concern. Once, at a posh gathering, his friends had to carry him from the room.

The observation that recurs in the letters and reminiscences of Schubert's friends is his relentless—yet almost effortless—escape from the bourgeois conventions of Viennese expectation, morality, and even law. Bauerenfeld remarks on Schubert's "genuine dread of commonplace and boring people, of philistines, whether from the upper or middle classes." "What is the good of a lot of quite ordinary students and officials to us?" Schubert asks. Another important intimate, Joseph von Spaun, saw his friend as "unusually frank, sincere, incapable of malice. . . . [but] not to be constrained by the conventions of society."

Schubert could be bored and frustrated even in the grand surrounds of the princely Esterházy family, where he accepted invitations to play and tutor on two separate occasions. "I sit here alone," he grumbled in a letter from the summer palace, "without having a single person with whom I could speak a sensible word." Because it was not wealth or comfort he sought but the communion of creative friends.

This tone of boredom and pique makes a sharp contrast to the persistent sentimental legend that Schubert harbored a romantic crush on the young Esterházy daughter Countess Karoline. It has been played up as quite the tearful thing, perfect for movies: the commoner's hopeless love of a princess. Yet the iconoclastic scholar Maynard Solomon has remarked on its unlikelihood, "for the countess was somewhat retarded—her mother sent her to play with her hoops when she was thirty."

If Schubert's own language and behavior are taken as evidence, it was not young ladies to whom he turned for love and companionship but to the men in his life. It was to Schober, with whom he lived first and last, moving in with him directly from his parents' house at nineteen, and again years later, in the months before his final illness. It was to the celebrated baritone Michael Vogl, twenty years his senior, who towered over him and took him traveling. It was, for a time, to that young Mortiz von Schwind mentioned by Bauerenfeld—whom Schubert (joking in earnest?) took to calling "my beloved." Schwind touchingly reported back to the absent Schober how intimately they were connected: "I share his whole life with him."

This side of Schubert is, as one would expect, never directly disclosed by his contemporaries. But his friends were forthright enough to affirm it in the negative. Anselm Hüttenbrenner declared Schubert's "dominating aversion to the daughters of Eve." Albert Stadler offered carefully that Schubert was "always rather reserved in this regard." Many others report the same thing.

Yet these same friends commented with remarkable unanimity on Schubert's "excessively indulgent sensual living" (as Schober put it), on his "double nature. . . . Inwardly a poet, and outwardly a kind of hedonist" (Bauerenfeld). Were they referring to the drinking and late hours? Or to sexual, possibly homosexual, license? Sober biographers tend to be agnostic.

But Schubert's musical contemporaries in the wider world seemed to be in on this open secret. Persistently, Schubert was belittled after his death as a kind of feminine shadow of more properly masculine composers. Robert Schumann (who otherwise seemed to idolize Schubert) saw him as "a maidenly character" compared to Beethoven:

> To be sure, he brings in his powerful passages, and offers massive sonorities; but he still always behaves like a woman to a man, who commands where she pleads and persuades.

Another complained: "Schubert's compositions are wearing thin. There is a certain coquetry, an effeminate weakness about them."

To say Schubert was "gay" would be to commit an anachronism. Neither the term nor the category existed, at least in the contemporary sense. What we do see is Schubert the escape artist. Schubert the hedonist, the drunk, the angel of song, the faithful friend who sometimes is nowhere to be found: Schwämmerl the uncontainable. Everything about him, from life to music, confounded the onlooker. Unless the onlooker was willing to let it in—to listen without barriers, to become, for a listening instant, as giddy and mercurial and openly feeling as the music itself. But that would be asking too much.

There is in every life a wide, deep layer of mushroominess, drawn from healthy but not altogether proper places. From soil, from paleness and dreaming, desire, darkness. Darkness that is not filth but is earthen and redolent of joy. Polished Imperial surfaces cannot cover it, cannot comprehend this planet's-worth of herebelow, for it is everywhere, an *umwelt*. From this source arises the bubbling brook and its glittering trout, the coruscating scherzo, the strange songs, the twists of sonatas: the mellow and the silly and the complex and the grieving—all the music, in other words, that no amount of money can buy, an irresistible wild upwelling.

It was Schubert's good sense not to resist it. But he resisted nearly everything else.

≡

When I was a teenager, starting to play a little better on the piano and sampling bits of Bach, Mendelssohn, Beethoven, and the like (but not yet Schubert), I loved Chopin best—the easiest of the preludes of course. And I seemed to play them a little less badly. Bach I adored listening to but could not play. It stymied me, this muscular, driving music. It seemed perfectly masculine: just what I ought to be but wasn't.

I listened to Bach hour after hour on vinyl records. I sought out organ concerts. In person I heard the C-minor *Passacaglia*, its bass drama my teenage drama. I contemplated fugues, flying and impossible, how they layered complexity upon difficulty and finally, in the *stretto* passage, drove all the darting and overlapping themes into a nearly unbearable tension. For me, Bach was a workshop in transcendence: flight, power, control, abandon.

But I couldn't play it. I now see that I had simply not put in the hours. And of course I was being ridiculous. Chopin's technical demands are legendary. Yet I felt exposed when I played his vividly emotional music in anyone's earshot. It was, simply put, too revealing—or too revealing for a closeted, desperate adolescent. I felt that I *should* have been playing Bach.

It seems absurd now. But it's how I lived the music. In fact it's how I lived everything, every minute of the day: caught in the trap of masculinity, what might be called the *straight-jacket*. My family culture was that hyper-masculine swirl of brothers, fathers, uncles, sports, competition. There really was nothing else. Even my evangelical Christianity was presented that way: as a distance race of grit and determination. *Don't give up. Don't give in to those weakling modernizers.* And the fundamental rule of masculinity was this: Do not feel. Be powerful. Act and do not be acted upon.

≡

Today, playing in the *studio de répétition*, Schubert's music moves me. It slips the straight-jacket, escapes, leaves home, lives in a land of feeling and expression and delight that I can experience myself, any time. Sometimes I travel to hear the Trout Quintet or the E-flat piano trio. In them, the inside is brought outside, expressed, exposed, brought to light where it glitters like the surface of that brook.

The critic Roland Barthes records a telling response to Schubert's music—his songs especially:

> The [music's] space is affective, scarcely socialized . . . its true
> listening space is, so to speak, *the interior of the head.*

What Barthes notices here is exactly my territory, the inner kinesthetics of an experiencing brain, that feeling just behind the eyes. Music resonates in the cave of consciousness, in some way mapping, measuring. And opening up, astonishingly, to public, shared experience.

Here is the shock and scandal of Schubert: a felt interiority suddenly becoming powerful and, what's worse, public. It is what the straight-jacket is designed expressly to prevent. It exemplifies what musicologist Lawrence Kramer calls the composer's "imaginary escape from the self-alienation, the emotional and sexual narrowness demanded of 'normal' men."

What is hidden and private, the inner life of intense emotion, becomes in the performance of Schubert's music a public sacrament of sensual liberation. It is so dangerous that a generation (and more) of music critics felt bound to distance themselves from it with the faint praise due to a dismissably "effeminate" composer. But Schubert will not stay dismissed. Schwämmerl shows up whenever, and wherever, he wants to.

Inner becomes outer. It's a moment of vertigo, a sublime confusion. This power of beauty, of creativity and emotion—what is it, that it dare to overcome the weight and constriction of men? Day by day I work on the sonata. It feels. It opens. Sometimes I do, too—when there's no one else to hear it.

⸺

A last word, after another month of secluded practice.

I have made friends with an American pianist, Lynne Mackey. In the *Cité*'s perfect little underground auditorium she performs contemporary American work with a breakneck cacophonous musicality: Robert Evett, Emma Lou Diemer, Amy Rubin. Lynne seems bulletproof, astonishing. Meeting her in the hallway one day, a little overawed, I joke about being on my way to abuse Schubert. "Oh, we've all done that," she smiles. It makes me feel better.

In time I angle closer to her. She's the real thing, and finally I give voice to my struggle with music performance: my inveterate freeze-up, my nerves, my shame. And she has a brisk, immediate answer. She's been there herself, I realize, as perhaps every performer has. "You have to replace the self-consciousness with something else. *You have to love the music.* Love it more. And when your mind starts to bother you, you just *go there.* Right into the music. The sound."

It is a complete answer, grounded, mushroomed, in the weightless gravity of sound and pleasure. In the months that follow, I try it. It feels like a path, like something I could learn to practice: loosening the straight-jacket, loving the music, making the sound more important than my clamoring ego. Letting it burgeon from within, that place that is pale and earthen and joyous.

Something begins to happen.

Beyond Goddard Canyon

Just a painted vase of flowers. A particular shade of blue.

It was at one of Paris's most beloved and (therefore) crowded museums. I had picked a midweek moment, walked over the river and down to the Musée D'Orsay and found I could get in without too much fuss. The nineteenth-century collection is easy to spoof: earnest Victoriana; deep-chinned pre-Raphaelytic maidens; Second-Empire vulgarity. And on the ground floor, a throng of oversized sculptural male nudes, jammed together like a too-crowded shower room at the gym. Weirdly alarming.

And still lifes—gawd, I've seen so many. In some way they are boredom personified: watching dried paint, petals that will never drop. Yet I am always attentive to them. I think of all those Low Country painters over at the Louvre, the exacting blooms, the tendrils and petals, sometimes even the beetles and slugs. They invite a life of patient looking. A quiet kind of reaching. But whence? And toward what?

══

Really it was not the flowers but the stippled blue background that got me: that Van Gogh ebullience of peri-corn-winkle-flower blue, dotty with paler hues a-dancing, and darker marks too, a violet subplot. All of it dazzling behind a simple pot of orange flowers with rather draggled petals, surrounded by leaves of evergreen-green. That's all.

But I see that blue, and my back-mind says, *There! There it is!* . . . and suddenly I am five thousand miles west fifteen years ago, boots cleating into frozen sand gritted between vertical plates of granite. I am breathing and taking another step, balancing my backpack carefully. Miles off trail, solo, climbing toward an unmarked notch in a ridge. I really can't afford an unbalanced moment.

Hand on the cold granite. Looking down. Looking up.

And there is the little friend, not five inches high. A tiny posy of five-petal flowers—Van-Gogh-blue, violet-blue—spherical on a tuby stem, above fresh frond leaves that hug the sand, between the granite and the left-over snow. Nodding, you know, ever so slightly. The slope is steep, not quite hand-over-hand, and there is the floweret practically at my face saying, hi. And . . . perhaps this is obvious, but it feels hard to convey: the poignancy, the intensity of a simple flower in a place like this. Such color, briefness, endurance. Around us on near cliffs are overlays of ice and snow, the implicit threat of change, rockfall, winter in seven-month freeze-ups. *What is beauty, then? What is flesh?* You might be tempted to ask.

But these are unbalancing questions. So I take a moment. A long moment. To clear my mind and go on.

As, perhaps, I should do also at the Musée D'Orsay. Someone else wants to look at the Van Gogh.

Blue flower mongering is an old, old literary trope, but I can't help it. I won't falsify the account just to mute the echo of Novalis. Or Gary Snyder. It's *my* flower: *Polemonium*. Called "sky pilot." A blue of the near void, infra-blue, violet, subversive, and subliminal: color of the air past sunset when the earth unrolls below you, the stars blaze early above. I used to shuffle the names together and say them out loud just to make conversation with myself: *Po-le-sky-moni-p-um-ilot*. It had a nice sound to it, alien, like *Rass-al-hahg-wee* the starname. Yes, I spoke it. And I got something back.

Beautifullest little flower. Woundable. Yet persisting. So may it be for us all.

When I resurface from this reverie I find I have been walking—my natural reflex for reflection—down the boulevard to the little footbridge (*Passarelle de Solférino*) and across to the grand gardens of the Tuileries. It is a raw day deep into February. But I have the tree-lined *allées* and squared-up parterres to myself. Bloomless, leafless, they expose the geometries of power, the delusions of official elegance: statues in deadeningly regular intervals all down the long gravel way and the odd curved rooves of the Louvre in the distance.

Beauty got a bad name here.

But still it hides out, ready to surprise. The naked human forms—despite their rote formalism—seem tender out here under the sky and wind. They do. Here is a naked boy bravely exposed, his legs resolutely planted, his arms flung wide protecting an enfeebled elder. His father, as it turns out.

The boy's brow is furrowed, his chin set in touching fierceness. A plaque tells me this is Spartacus; this is his legendary resolve. The useless courage of a twelve-year-old.

All the white-marble limbs are perfect. Even the old man is handsome. Is it beauty that touches me so suddenly? I can't quite say. No one wants to be caught staring at little boys. But something of my own story is here, surely: that original attempt to discover what will be sufficient to stand in this world. Everyone's story is here, in some way.

A perfect boy. A perfect old man. Exposure, impossibility. A failing beauty.

≡

On High Sierra topo maps I had found an isolated stream high up in the backcountry. From a lake ringed with peaks it ran for about two miles along its own little dashing and pausing course before abruptly plunging a couple thousand feet into the south fork of a famous river. The unnamed valley was walled with steeps on both sides. Its headwall formed a classic cirque, glacier-carved, solid and sheer. No trail came in on any side. None.

On previous summers I had explored the approaches. Nothing doing from the north or the east. South out of the question. But then I found a granite ridge with a single notch like a missing tooth. Walked up to reconnoiter from a far-below campsite, lightly equipped. Stood in the gap looking down. Planned it all out in my mind. Wondered how the downclimbing would go with a full backpack. Or the upclimbing, for that matter. About 12,500 feet.

And here I was the next summer, actually doing it. Getting flowered as I arose, light-headed, to try the gap and see what would happen.

≡

I stayed a week, finding what I had hoped to find: Jeffrey pine and lodgepole. Alders on the river. Slick-rock creek, bounding, hiding, revealing its long green pools. Stars rising and falling over silhouette ridges. Everything, everything, everything. Sometimes my heart felt like bursting. Other times, I played my harmonica like a movie scene of loneliness, no one to hear it by the fire.

Mornings I looked at plants, poring over my dichotomous key that sometimes could track down family, genus, species. Or not, if I made a wrong turn. It was slow work, perfect for patience beneath a latecoming sun that found, at last, the shadowed valley.

Some days I went to sit above the trees and look out from stonefells and glacier-smoothed heights, amid that famous Sierra granite that went white-bright in the noon but glowed rose and gold in the dawn and evening twilight. After a few days, when I was rested, I tried scrambling up the headwall above the top lake. But it proved too steep to be a way out, at least without the safety of a hiking partner. I was secretly content with that: I would leave the same way I had entered. No more unknowns. My little land in the sky, my solitary confinement, my wondering-place, my finding-place.

Sometimes I feel like a pomegranate so full of these translucent moments that they might spill out if I am bumped too hard.

Then I go back to my normal rough-skinned self. But I remember. I think about what I have within me, what has been given. That abundance.

One day I heard a helicopter booming, probably out over the big down-there river where a road full of tourists came shuttling in and out to play and walk. It was an ominous sound, loud, everywhere, hard to track. Somebody in trouble, being rescued. Or some *body* being taken back, too late. Or someone, on a trail or resting at a lake, who needs to be found, to be told bad news.

I thought of my dear partner, back in our house in Los Angeles. How I had kissed him, and held him, and told him what ranger station to call if I didn't check in by our agreed time. How I told him I was coming back, no damage, no drama; in fact, I promised it. I was very stubborn about that. Hiking solo meant making no dumb moves. I knew the risks, and I knew how to pare them down to nearly nothing. Nearly. I *would* walk out: that was my commitment. No accidents.

But what if someone else had had an accident?

Alone, your thoughts can spool and spin.

Nights, I built fires. Days, I wrote about the mountains. About love. About having found a safe place in my life at forty, at last, with the man I thought I would be with forever. Tried not to let melodrama invade my peace. Resisted its everywhere-fears with the peace of place. Fished and fished and fished.

Those were geological trout.

They had been here in deep time, coming up the glacial meltwaters, swimming through turquoise pools, bounding up spring freshets and sum-merlong cascades, up and up into naked tarns that had spent the previous ten or fifty or a hundred thousand years resisting the bottomweight of gla-ciers, getting a good grinding, a gouging and then a polishing, as if preparing for trout to come. There is evidence that the cutthroat trout and its forebears have been around these parts for a million years. However they look, that's how this place looks. However they move, that's how this place moves.

The skin of a cutthroat is slick, like local granite: water-smooth, glacier-smooth. Stone-cool to the hand, too, as I extract the mouth-hooking terror and whack the fish on a jagged boulder edge just at the base of the brain, as quick and final as I can. It suffers for a less-than-geological moment, that is true. Life, not-life. It's the business we are all in.

The color of a cutthroat is subtle, mysterious in the watery glimpse and in the hand amazing, intricate. You might think that some meaning was locked up there, a pattern to read—like trying to read the rock history, that jumble of pressure and fire and interruption, stories so intricate that neither imagination nor science can follow them all. You're left with a rock in the hand, a fish in the hand, a small weight of wondering. Why these hues, these freckles and bands? Why the pale-scarlet cutthroat thumb-smudge on either side the neck, the wash of pink down the belly, the delicate green of the back all dotted with black?

No reason, every reason. Necessity the blind artist, sculptor of form. Life and death. The business we're all in.

I'll eat him later ("him" because no eggs as I run my thumbnail down the backbone, scooping the viscera into a hole kicked in the duffy soil, red-pink-black jewels in the dust). His meat will be pink and firm from a stream-dweller's slimming diet of mosquitos. It will flake in my all-purpose plastic cup, and the butter I treasure and cool in the stream to drop into the tiny frying pan will translate the skin and tail and fine pectoral fins to a transparent crispness that seems beyond luxury, ten days into this hidden place. Protein, pleasure, the fat, the crunch.

━

I'm sitting out the rest of the morning on the sunny side of a bend in the creek, where shallows are dabbed with wet-footed plants. I know this sort of scene well enough: brief meadowed flat, pale stones embedded in short grasses that overlap the pool at an undercut edge, pinky-blue lupine around as always, as everywhere, though just a dwarf version at this elevation. On the shady side, tall orange tiger lilies with curved leaves halfway up like hands on hips. Jeff pine surrounding my two-yard meadow, tall and safemaking behind me. It's a good spot for a human.

In the sedgy edges, my eye is drawn to the favorite flower: Sierra shooting star. It's a tiny intense-pink comet, petals swooping back from the neck as if under a motionless acceleration behind a little thrusting prow. High drama, hardly an inch across. Rimmed in yellow to contrast with the tiny aerodynamic leading spar all sooty-black with pollen. More than a dozen in the bright-pebbled shoal.

The sunshine moves, mottled shade and bright gaps shifting. The stream shifting. The peaks around seeming not to shift, but they do. I know they do. I am warm in my spot, rocketing motionlessly through beauty. Beauty. Beauty I cannot name or grasp. Only the moment, the curl of water around a stone fallen from somewhere, somewhen. Mudbeauty. Stick-and-twig-beauty.

Only the moment. I can't call it "sublime" because it's just me with my pants a little damp in the grassy seat, just me among the sedges and marvels. Where is the vastness, that heart-dropping spin of terror and delight, that behind-the-forehead infinity like a dizziness of too much real?

Just this streamside. The ache of the temporary. If I remember my Edmund Burke correctly, this would be called *the Beautiful*, in pale contrast to *the Sublime*. But I see plainly that the sublime is no opposite to the beautiful.

Beauty, I think, is just vastness foregrounded by delicacy.

≡

The warrant for refusing to separate the sublime from the beautiful lies within Edmund Burke's work itself. Almost anyone who reads the famous tome notices that Burke does not write much about the truly beautiful, despite his title. What he contrasts to the sublime is really *the pretty*. Gamely he praises the neat, the tidy, the smooth, orderly, well-crafted, and controlled. It's actually a bit comical how limp and uninteresting he leaves "beauty"— presumably the better to magnify the majesty of the sublime.

But beauty is too important to leave tarted up and dumbed down on the side of the road like this. Beauty too leaves us charged and mute as it passes. Not the whirlwind but the whisper. Not the spectacle but the quietly alluring. A rose, a face, a scent that carries us beyond. What, and whence, we cannot say.

An Englishman who lived a century before Burke gave us a truer account. Francis Bacon, in his essay "Of Beauty," offered this durable motto: "There is no excellent beauty that hath not some strangeness in the proportion." I've been carrying those words in my heart for decades now, calling them up to help me in moments when beauty seems almost too upsetting in its distant call and close demand, when the very air seems charged with some unformulated question, unexpectedly taking you up, up, when you're otherwise just bumbling along in your life.

Once "strangeness" is admitted, the beautiful becomes again a thing of power and mystery. Becomes, in other words, a precinct of the sublime. Bacon again: "Beauty itself is but the sensible image of the infinite." You could say that the sublime is the country wherein the beautiful lives, though out at the calmer edges. The higher peaks and snowy crags of sublimity are never out of sight, and the waters of terror run through them all. Look deeply and the beautiful, too, will chill. Will leave you restless, unprepared, unfinished.

To collapse Burke's neat duality, to reacquaint the beautiful with the sublime, is to bring the scale of wonder back home, back to our hearts and lives—not to relegate it as a thing of rare moments and extraordinary locales. It is to reinhabit largeness, depth, and scope as necessary components of a felt and thoughtful life: a life constantly recharged by a deeper vitality.

This is real food for the spirit. Bread that does not perish. Inexpressibly more than the meager condiments of religiosity or politics or pleasure seeking; the stacking up of money; the accumulation of renown. Those are wood hay and stubble, as we used to say at church. Inedible, negligible, burned up in the passage of a day.

But a passage of beauty or a moment of awe: these never cease to nourish.

—

Everyone knows the paradox of beauty: that pressure in the eyes, that catch in the throat. A feeling of tears, even in the midst of pleasure. As if joy were incomplete without sorrow.

I do believe it is possible not to notice these things. To live determinedly on the surface. To *not go there*. Understandably, because it's not safe there. Feelings beyond words. Realities deeper than we can plumb. Keeping things pretty is always an option, staying in the orderly and well known. People do.

But the poet Wallace Stevens insists that there is no beauty without the deeper dangers: "Death is the mother of beauty." Over and over he says it, in his strange and gnomic way. Because beauty perishes, as we do, there is no beauty that is not somehow touched with death, change, time. And because what is beautiful is precious, we feel it keenly, that impendingness. Beauty lives only in the least-durable dimension, the one that breaks our hearts.

It seems to me that the beautiful is the tick of time, as the sublime is the scale of space.

The Sierra shooting star nods in a slant of afternoon sun. I have brought a hand lens with me, but I won't dissect. Not this time. In a week the blooming may be over. In a week I will certainly be departed. The August creek will fall, the meadow will brown; then snows will fill in and freeze their own killing beauty into the scene, frightening. Sublime no doubt. No one to see it, but I feel it anyway.

It is a dangerous bargain we make, to admit these experiences into our hearts. The mortal boundedness of beauty: *nothing that we love will stay*. And the unboundedness of the sublime: *we live amidst inexpressible forces*. And in some way we cannot comprehend, these twin infinitudes have conspired to produce . . . *us*.

Whatever can it mean? We cannot come to the end of feeling this thought, thinking this feeling. And this is the best a living being can experience: trembling, at once filled and empty, on the brink of wonders.

—

My thought life scaling old mountains, all the riches of Europe around me. I love these days of wandering, seeing, remembering. But it is a strange way to be in Paris.

St. Eustache II: The Sound World

January—

With an otherworldly shock, the sound that meets me as I push into the building is an almost physical pressure: sound like oceans, like waterfalls, like waves rolling and over-rolling themselves. I stand a moment, red-cheeked from my rush across the wintery Paris morning, to de-hat and de-scarf just within the side door. The music tumbles on, fugue-like, treble ringing and bass billowing, up to the chancel end then back in reverberation, re-crossing in overtones, undertones, dissonances at the confused edge of hearing—color, roil, and trouble—the pell-mell push of melody keeping its head above water, barely. Bravely.

My eyes have hardly adjusted to this gray-lit interior, but my ears have already measured it. A sonic model of the space builds in my hearing, in my head. It is wide, deep, worthy. Seconds into St. Eustache, I am almost instantly expanded into it by sound. As if the whole space were mine, were me. It's a big feeling; I admit it.

This is exactly what I remember from my first visit, a few years ago. Last week it was just the silent, light-crossed building, a weekday. Today I don't know if I'll stay for Mass. But I'm glad I'm here now.

===

Jean Guillou sits at the huge show console of the organ at the back end of the vaulted nave amid chairs and onlookers. I know there must be another console up high, out of sight among the pipes, but this one can be rolled out in full view. Every Sunday before the Mass he offers this sound carnival, this spectacle, this feast of wordless blessing. There's a crowd to see him, seated and standing.

He's in full flight as I make my way down the wide stone side aisle, survey the crowd, slip into a seat. He is silver haired and lithe as a dancer in his tailored suit of light blue and his tight, shiny pumps. Feet swinging and touching, fingers arms shoulders in perpetual motion, head bent or erect, absorbed yet above it all at the same time, he is the very image of mastery. Gives me a chill: the sound that never ceases, the complications he threads with such ease. Ease, difficulty, and grace. Instantly he becomes my new old friend, and in my mind I take to calling him *Jean*.

He commands four keyboards and a pedalboard, plus a semicircle array of stops, pistons, presets—some down there by his feet. At the right instant his hand flicks, or his toe tips, and he engages this set of pipes, disengages that, links some others together. My eyes rise to the gunmetal-gray organ pipes behind him, serried and staged almost to the ceiling high above the west entrance. Barrel-wide basses and shining diapasons flank sweeps of smaller and smaller pipes and tubes and flutes and pencil-tiny piccolos, rank upon rank. A massive blond-wood buffet frames it all, topped by carved figures, *David* right and *St. Eustache* left, their graceful wooden *contrappostos* strangely tender amid the sleek verticals of steel and antimony.

Towering. Theatrical. Almost kitschy, like most organ pipe displays—promising the world. But this one delivers.

The fugue rolls on toward its finish, powerful and strangely empowering. I feel the uplift, the drama of Jean's performance, so flawless and brave. The music is muscular but lush, luscious. In the folded program I see why: it is Robert Schumann's tribute to Bach, playing on the letters of his name (spelled out in the German style of notation). So I'm hearing a romantic's idea of a fugue. It has roared, now it sighs. I'm a romantic myself half the time, and I like it.

It ends and there's a pause for the last chord to finish its journey and leave us in a sort of high-calorie silence, silence embodying everything, carved from nothing. It's an odd, destabilizing feeling, that long beat of after. So—too soon—we fill it with applause. Jean twists around on the bench and half-bows. He acknowledges us, pauses, turns back to the keyboard. Then we wait—a breath, two breaths, three . . . and he is off to the races, improvising for the last five minutes before Mass. Improvisation used to be a standard skill for church organists, but it astonishes modern audiences. Jean knows the instrument, he knows the hall. Decades ago he himself oversaw the rebuilding of the organ. Now, in the moment, he manipulates it all, sound and space, delay and immediacy. It's a fever dream, a revelation, a *débauche*. St. Paul on the road to Damascus; *Queen* on the road to oblivion.

Who knows what disturbances or what solaces this congregation of strangers takes from it. Me, I'm here. Simply here. Here the present is made tangible, bigger than ever, a good place to be.

Jean hits a huge chord, all ten fingers and both feet. You can feel the bass in your chest and arms and seat. He sends the burst hurtling forward into the vaulted space and then lifts himself off the keys—hands in the air, feet suspended. In the long pause, the sound rolls out and returns three seconds, four seconds older, richer by nooks and niches, by windows and groins and arches: enriched, engaged, and returned. The long reverb. The big space. He knows how it works.

More than any other instrument except perhaps the human voice, a pipe organ lives only in its building, its true body. The best organ in a space too echoey or too small is but a poor organ. Without a suitable sonic medium, the organ is like a violin fretboard without its warm curvy scrollwork body. The organ's sound, its deep rolling booms and massing chords and sharp cries like trumpets, like harpies, like hosannas, simply cannot happen without room to breathe, to build and bloom and die away. The building is the body. And we, of course, are *inside* it.

Imagine being inside Joshua Bell's Stradivarius violin. There. Feel that?

And of all organs and their buildings, St. Eustache must be among the most perfectly matched. I have heard many. This is the best.

I have read speculation that the human experience of "now" amounts to the buffering speed of our brain system, and that this is roughly 3.5 seconds. That would be the duration of our sense of the present: the moment we live in, before it slides into the past. (Others think it might be as long as seven seconds or even a full minute.) This is a paradoxical duration: William James, the philosopher, called it the "specious present" since it is actually composed of "earlier" and "later" moments—yet these are somehow felt to be all *now*.

The time signature of this space is three to four seconds from inception to reverberation to silence. This is the "now" of St. Eustache, while the organ plays. While I listen. While voices echo. It produces an at-rest feeling. Perhaps there is a comfort of self-recognition in this acoustic temporality: our ears, our bodies, our minds. Our time being.

February—
I'm here early, silent on my habitual seat in the transept. I know there will be Bach, but before him the elusive Couperin: antique, charming . . . I never

feel I quite know him. My shoulder bag rests on the floor, full of poetry and politics to read, a big lab notebook to write in. But I'm just sitting here. Somehow I'd rather just wait.

The *bee-bahh bee-bahh* of a Euro-siren wafts in, close enough to hear the Doppler change as it wails by. When that's gone I begin to hear whisper-talking from some tourists, shutter-clicks and then boot heels tapping away to another side chapel. I know what they're looking at: there is the statue of Rameau. By it is the crypt of that obscene financier whose tactics supported some Louis or other. They'll see the oil by Rubens, dimmed by time and rather offhand placement in a dark corner. And close by that, the Keith Haring altarpiece, silver-bright and contemporary amid the dust of centuries. If they keep going they will see that uncomfortably coy Virgin in the lady chapel with her candlelit devotees. I know these things; I have watched and whispered them myself.

Noisy onlookers are as resident here as mute artworks and ancient objects. What else is human space but busy byplay, overlay, interruption? The moil of the group, twitching and gossiping. But noises are not interruptions if you don't take them that way, I think to myself (I seem to be calmer and less judgmental than usual). A dog, probably belonging to one of the homeless guys, barks out on the plaza. Vendors clatter faintly, unloading their trucks for market in the street. A phone inevitably chimes close by.

All sound is present at once. Unlike the ever-choosing, ever-focusing eye, the ear does not choose; "where the eye divides, the ear connects," says the composer John Luther Adams. Sound is translucency and depth, like looking downward into clear, deep water. Sound beneath, sound above. This big space takes it all in and returns it with something additional: something like silence slides in between the noises. Or even, within them. A kind of spacey permissiveness.

The sound world is a realm of expansion and patience.

I experiment with expansion and patience.

⸺

A walk in the woods can teach it, too. This I am led to think about often, I who carry my busy-mindedness like a burden (and who doesn't?), the darting thought-life so overeager to know and control and fill every instant with discrimination. Where I come from there are forests rather than cathedrals, and they suffice. So in the heart of Paris I remember the Salmon River Trail and the old grove I love to come upon just a half mile in, where

the river curves and leaves the place intact (for now), a place heavy with
mosses and crisscrossed with downed timber floored or leaning against the
old, old verticals of hemlocks and firs, vast and reliable, taller than eye can
see from down in the redolent green pocket, their swaying liminal, forgotten and then felt, remembered. It's another world, echoing and spacious.
The sound is river. Is air moving through treetops unseen. Is breath and
breathing.

There comes quietness, expansion. Many-dimensionality.

Paul Shepard, the anthropologist and ecologist, speaks feelingly of "the
sound world." He was my great teacher, though I only met him once. In his
books he often returns to a particular state of awareness, a "quality of attention" difficult to achieve in the striving linearity of the city, but in woods and
deserts quite literally natural. Shepard draws on the Spanish philosopher
José Ortega y Gassett, whose book *Meditations on Hunting* describes these
contrasting states of mind. "Merely to look . . . is to direct the sight to a point
in the surroundings. . . . being absorbed in one point of the visible area and
not paying attention to the other points," says Ortega. However:

> The hunter's look and attention are completely opposite to
> this . . . It is a "universal" attention, which does not inscribe itself
> on any point and tries to be on all points. There is a magnificent
> term for this, one that still conserves all its zest of vivacity and
> imminence: alertness. The hunter is the alert man.

In this attentiveness, vision becomes more like hearing. The "alert man," or
woman, employs field-awareness, not point-awareness, taking everything in
democratically. It is a different mentality, alert yet relaxed, receptive. Seeing
as if taught by hearing.

Entering the sound world we can be canny as hunters—real hunters,
not shooting from helicopters or stalking penned-in game victims but waiting on the edges of clearings, trusting to what the world may bring, relying
on the world's abundance. The frantic constricting scarcity of capitalism, the
striving self-promotion of city life are left behind. "Here" is the waiting soul,
attentive to the all-around, aware in all directions.

The noticing self, ready for gifts to be given.

The Couperin begins.

March—
Today there will be Bach. Much Bach.

Before I have time to think the organist charges into the "Prelude in D Major," launching this bright, faintly martial key with an eight-note ascent and four confidently slower answering chords: ONE-TWO-THREE-FOUR! It repeats, for the pleasure of it. Then, evermoving, we are dropped into softer voices and far less certainty. The path of the music is wandering, asking, way-finding. Moments are discovered then lost in shadow. I follow the music, the sound. Lost and found in it.

But where, exactly, am I? What is this place? There is a domed present-ness in music: a large, connected, but open space within which to think, experience, feel.

For me music is the pattern for all the arts, the epitome. In music I am most present. I am participant and witness at the same moment: music becomes inside me as it sounds outside me. I can feel this happening, and it brings emotion, connectedness, thought that is *almost but not quite* rational thought—"thought" that might follow its own path, you know how thinking is. Yet music is not thought. It is experience.

Listening to Jean as he takes us forward—my head floating, my body and mind entrained and alert—it seems to me that music is a simulacrum of the brain, or more properly, of mind. And that within it, we think in an expanded self. Every work of art (that succeeds) offers us this unlimited experiential space. We think *through* and *in* and *by means of* the music. The poem. The story, sculpture, theater piece, dance.

Every art seeks to create this kind of dimensional think-space. I'm call-ing it: *conscious space*. For me, it's easiest to apprehend in music. Best of all if the music's physical locale is large, itself a model of the mind in its dome of fragile bone.

The prelude comes to its confident close. After long minor-key per-plexity, the conclusion toggles upward in that familiar way, saving the day in the very last chord (a "Picardy third" is the technical name—you'd know it if you heard it). The chord calls out, echoes, dies away. This is shared space, resonant, unifying.

≡

All my life I have carried this readiness with me, within me. Hasn't everyone? A kind of ache that echoes and responds when the music suddenly floats in from the next room or the next alley, when the light slants just so, when the fragrance arises from the vine or the baker's open window, when the passing stranger's glance seems suddenly emotional, personal. And the heart leaps up, as if it were waiting all along for this, just this.

It's like we are the children of Israel, bringing our tabernacle with us. Setting it up at a moment's beckoning. Dwelling there, in the instant, like saints of receptiveness and beauty.

Before, next moment, going back to honking and cursing and making a living.

≡

This is the thought experiment of St. Eustache.

That *music is the mind's moveable kiva*. That it both *represents* and *is* consciousness. That we know ourselves in it and come to know existence through it. More than mirror in its layered translucency, music is a hall of mirrors, echoing and representing ourselves in ways that add dimension, surprise, depth, beauty. The mind apparently craves this self-representation.

A holy space (kiva, cathedral, ritual cave, sacred grove . . .) both represents the world and is the world. It is a sacred metaphor, an enactment where the crucial gestures may be played out on behalf of the whole. In the kiva the world must be renewed every year, and the kiva space is regularly reentered, weekly and daily. So the conscious space of music must always be reentered, reenacted, re-heard. It is like water: we drink for today, for now. Tomorrow we drink again.

I find music to be a daily necessity, like dinner with friends or walking. My human life is incomplete, flat, and unsatisfying without music woven into the daily texture. Best if it is *live* music, wrought from nothing, just humans playing into the shared void, creating space and movement and connection, then letting it disappear.

In the fullness of music—of any art experienced—there is a rounded satisfaction, however fleeting. In the fractured world, here is order. In the weary brokenness of life, here is wholeness. It restores our soul.

≡

This shared space created by music, what is it?

To me it strongly suggests other big spaces: the night sky, the high arbor of a swaying grove. I believe it is the dome of the skull, the habitation of mind. Emily Dickinson famously said that she knows it's poetry when it makes you feel like the top of your head has come off. *That's it.* That's the moment when you have entered art-mind, music-mind, poetry-mind—when your brain space has become shockingly wider, deeper. Your eyes get big and round when this happens. You enter a state of heightened awareness. Connection seems to be everywhere, surprising you. Delighting you. Blessing you.

It is meaningful space, *conscious* space: soulish, shared, sacred.

The caverns of paleolithic art seem to present this experience exactly. In the caves of southern France and northern Spain—Chauvet, Altamira, and perhaps a few dozen others—we are lucky to be able to see truly ancient representations of this experience. When I stood in the limestone darkness of Font de Gaum or of Peche Merle, perhaps I saw what our forbears saw: an evocation of shared mind, of consciousness itself. Perhaps.

The dome of the cavern can be experienced as the dome of the mind—externalized, concretized, and thus made both more knowable (via the senses) and more unknowable—because there's more going on than can be fathomed. Animal drawings flicker, motionlessly moving. Sound echoes. The coolness of the cave on the skin, the clean, damp smell in the nose. Dust, charcoal. Probably, for the original users, singing or chanting. The cave offers collaboration with physicality, like the mind's with the body, that is never resolved, never resolvable. Its echoes and interactions might go on forever. *Have* gone on forever, you could say—thirty or forty thousand years, which for our kind would be a fair version of "forever."

We are temporary beings full of memory and vastness. In a sacred cave, sacred grove, sacred space, we know it. Sound may build this consciousness around us, and within us, briefly. When it passes, we are joyful grievers.

~

I wonder if the fire-circle was not perhaps the first conscious space. A gold-yellow presence lights faces and bodies; it glints in the eyes of fellow humans, those you love and fear, those with whom you sleep and eat and breathe every day. We lived like this for several hundred thousand years: a small group, maybe twelve to twenty-five people. A life of finding food, killing it, trying to stay safe. Firelight flickers up tree branches, paints the rocks around, brightens insects flying through. The space is defined, a little golden dome of humanity.

Above us arcs the greater dome, starry. Both move, seem to have histories, behaviors. When I have sat huddled among my fellow humans, it felt like this. Weeks and months in the backcountry, the Sierras, North Cascades, Smokies, Rockies. Deserts and wild shorelines, too. Always the little pocket of warmth in the big big world, stars wheeling overhead.

My buddy Bob is quietly singing, his calm baritone full of reassurance. His guitar, his voice . . . that's all it takes. He's skinny as a reed, has a drawn, bearded, nearly chinless face and funny intelligent brown eyes. Under our sky, we pitch this little habitation of warmth, of solidarity, sung against the cold settling down from the peaks, the fatigue of the day, the practice of fragility that underwrites all climbing and striving. All living.

He lifts up his voice. Yellow light encircles us. He sings into the dark, and we grow larger in the singing. Even years later, when friendship has broken and time has made me weak, I can remember this. I can sit, solitary, and access it. Moveable, portable, rememberable. A small shiver runs up my back, and even in solitude I am not alone.

Music is the mind's moveable kiva. We can erect the dome of simplicity and splendor with nothing but a few strums, a practiced voice, a fullness that grows in the space of a breath. A memory. A sound. We do it daily, weekly. We renew ourselves.

Consciousness is spatial—that is, the *experience* of consciousness (and what else is it, but an experience?). It's what I feel, and have felt, times beyond counting: mountains and woods, seashore and sunset, painting poetry music. The mind suddenly more than you think. More than you *can* think.

This volume and spatiality is what the sublime is all about. The release, the challenge, the emptying, the strange tingling fullness of fear and delight. In my life, it has been the essential counterweight, the great answer to all narrowness, all doctrine, all self-hatred, all politics and cant and bloodshed and fearing.

It is the greater mind that we all share. It is how we get to our larger self.

Jean Guillou follows the Bach with improvisation as wandering as a mountain trail. Later, I know, the choir will sing more Bach, voices human and blending: *Ruth wohl*, they will sing. *Repose en paix* translates the program: rest well and be at peace. Our voices, our moment, this human space containing everything. And nothing: just sound, about to disappear.

Schubert III: Changing My Mind

Schubert pushes me off balance.

Day by day I approach the keyboard with my small store of determination. I sit, look at the notes, push away that sense of shameful ineptness that tries to silence me. I breathe in. Here are the sonorous chords—see? These I can touch, my long fingers go around them easily. And here, the lilting course of the tale. So I begin.

But just as I rest in some easy rhythm or happy melody, ready to linger there, Schubert tosses the action into the other hand, or syncopates it, or steers it into another key. Soon he leaves that moment behind too, another pearl fallen on the trail, while sharp new turns and difficulties arise. Measure by measure, I encounter simple-seeming patterns—pleasant and uncomplicated to hear—that are, how to say it, just weirdly off-putting to actually play.

This morning I find myself staring at another handful of defeating measures. I tell myself, it's just a few descending notes against a steady right hand. Or, just two beats against three, that familiar trope. Yet woven into them is a devilish habit of going the opposite way from whatever is obvious, going where the hand and eye don't expect to go, and in fact don't *want* to go. Exactly there, page after page, the off beat, the off kilter, hard as hobnails to play. And yet always it *sounds* right. Sounds inevitable, in fact.

Schubert draws a silken pleasantness out of difficulty. In my experience, Schubert on the piano is seldom harrowing or intellectual. He is well and deeply felt, of course, and often delighting—interesting, always. But never really brow furrowing. It's not intellectual music; it's *music* music. I can only conclude that the concealed difficulties are, in fact, a prime source of Schubert's evergreen freshness. It's why Schubert and not Salieri. Or not Hummel. Those worthies are eminently fluid, correct, sometimes even inventive. But we're not drawn to listen and relisten, are we?

They lack the demons.

The old word *daemon* used to mean a kind of driving spirit, a powerful force that might lurk in the heart of the woods or the heart of a person. Not evil, but not safe, either. Demons change things. They switch signs, get you lost, confuse you. Coyote, Loki, Puck. They are tricksters and troublemakers, laughing *not quite kindly* at your human frailty. A kind of low comedy can result—banana peel, switcheroo, wrong door, wrong sweetheart—and like all slapstick, it is never far from cruelty. "Panic," after all, is named after Pan, the goat-legged god, the nature spirit who disorients wood wanderers, who watches their consternation sharpening from anxiety to fear to pell-mell blindness, headlong rushing, catastrophe. He leaves behind an eerie green calm with its echo of laughter.

I have been tangled in forests, confounded in mountains. I have seen Pan's face, or sensed it anyway, just around the next boulder, next drop-off, false summit, fatal mistake. I have talked out loud to him (to me): *Slow now; stop now; drink water; breathe.* And then, when I had calmed myself enough to continue, he would keep his distance. Not far off, you understand. He would be watching.

Here in the faery woods of Schubert, something similar. For I am prone to panic when I find myself in a fast and changeful passage. If I feel eyes watching, an audience of any kind, then I begin to watch myself and suddenly it becomes worse: my upper mind distracts with whispered thoughts, irrelevant, critical, wordy, and suddenly I'm not truly *playing*, which like all games requires presence and alertness. Then it's all low comedy, clatter and clash. Exactly like someone who is distracted and flustered and cannot even watch where his feet are going, tripping on roots and rugs.

Tiring, really, to be the butt. So in my time of Paris abundance, my time-out-of-time in the wilds of the metropolis, I slow down. Practice becomes *a practice*. Gradually, the mental chatter abates, and . . . oh so incrementally . . . I develop a sturdier kind of calm. And there is the maxim from my pianist friend Lynne to guide me now: *love the music.* More than anything else this keeps me on the path. My shoulders relax into the pleasure of the sound.

It is slow work. Sometimes I feel a listening nearby, a charged field, a presence: impish, amused. I'm learning to let it watch.

＝

Demons change things. And I believe that whosoever enters the Schubert must emerge changed, too.

Maybe this is just a highfalutin way of stating the obvious: that learning is changing. After a lifetime of teaching, I can report that a student resistant to change is no student. Every classroom has a few of this sort. They sit in the back, daydreaming, doodling, uninterested. Fidgety, yet deeply inert. They are studies in being stuck, usually conservative or even reactionary in their unfiltered responses (should the teacher actually pry any out): slogans, set phrases, prejudices. Without some willingness to change, they are unreachable.

Because to learn anything is to change the mind, at least a little. And this must mean changing the brain. Whether inserting an isolated fact or comprehending a grand philosophic theme, whether learning dance steps or differential equations—something actual changes in the brainstuff. It must.

This is what the neurobiologists, empowered by new imaging technology, have begun to study. The brain in action shows up on a screen: neural activity *here* and *here*, a physical illumination. Electric. I have begun reading monographs and reports: amygdala, cerebellum ... It's a bit much to follow. But the message is clear, seen in its physicality as never before. However the mind works, its brain learns by physical changes in its circuitry. Whatever region gets used most shows up as circuit-rich, engorged and electrified, and often physically larger.

Oliver Sacks's book *Musicophilia* offers us civilians some easy views of this new work. He reports, for instance, that the neuroscientist Gottfried Schlaug and his associates have been investigating the brains of musicians since the mid-1990s, finding that several structures are noticeably enlarged and in a way that instantly identifies a musician: the corpus collosum (connecting the brain's hemispheres) and other parts of the brain related to auditory and—interestingly—spatial perception and response. Meanwhile another researcher, Alvaro Pascual-Leone, has found that the brain "can show changes within minutes of practicing."

Minutes! I feel encouraged already.

═

But I think there's more: a more comprehensive version of this insight. Yes, to learn is to change. But what changes is, potentially, *everything*. To shift one thing in a neural web is to change relationships, unpredictably and in any direction, non-linearly, like twanging a web. And a brain is fundamentally a web of connectivity. The linking is all.

But weblike organization can be challenging to think about. Like phre-nologists of old, we really want to *locate* each important feeling or skill in one definable place: *here it is*. But the reality may be more complicated and elusive. More Puckish, perhaps. Professor Lisa Feldman Barrett of North-western University has performed a wide-ranging meta-analysis (surveying and collating results of numerous other studies), to look for evidence of spe-cific brain regions or structures associated with specific experiences. But her result is surprisingly null: no correlation. The brain, Barrett finds, constructs experiences in ways that are highly dispersed. The whole network, or a large portion of it, seems to engage even on basic emotions like fear or anger. It's an interestingly subtle point: Schlaug had found that our skills develop specific brain structures. But our experience, more broadly, disperses across the whole thing. It appears to be a point that's unsettled, perhaps a little unsettling. It's above my head to try to adjudicate the difference.

Yet it seems that dropping a new fact or experience into the still pool of the mind might send ripples or waves almost anywhere. Small changes can vibrate elements unpredictably distant in the web of thoughtful neurons. For systems (as Gregory Bateson liked to insist) respond *systematically* to input. They aren't billiard tables bouncing out a bit of linear momentum. Neural systems, living systems, react according to their own inner logic. They *decide*, even on the neuronal level. They amplify, dampen, layer; they add or subtract energy at each node. There are perhaps 100 billion neurons in a brain, as Daniel J. Levitan observes, and the number of possible combinations "ex-ceeds the number of known particles in the entire known universe." When you start rearranging things, the result goes far beyond predictability. It's a starry pool aswirl with possibility.

To leap from the cellular to the holistic, who has not occasionally found life pivoting on some single thing, insignificant in itself, that opened up a world? A word, a sound, a chance encounter, a single thought whose consequence reverberated in strange and long-lasting ways.

Nonlinear. Strange-looped. Spooky, perhaps. Things happen to us that *are* us, taking shape deep within our being, out of sight, according to our own systems of responding. One well-connected researcher (Dr. Stuart R. Hameroff of the Center for Consciousness Studies) says simply: "Consciousness is more like music than computation." The way it adds up is always more than a simple sum of parts. Like a melody, perhaps: why is one unforgettable—"Ave Maria" or "Take the A Train"—while another is flat and forgotten?

It's a mystery. So far.

≡

Today it's the sonata's third movement, that Scherzo. The word means "joke" and usually implies a fast-paced levity, though sometimes the humor gets a little rough ("almost savage" says my Oxford music dictionary). Like any good joke, it's all in the timing. Fast fast fast. I doubted, when I undertook it, that my left hand would actually be able to learn that pattern, learn it well enough to repeat it all day, while trading the lead with the right like two jugglers tossing brightness to each other, unhesitating, seamless, laughing. Yet I did. It sparkles like water in a fountain. I am, frankly, amazed to hear it.

Show up. Still your mind. Do the work. Breathe.

Here is what I can report. Sometimes in my life and body I can feel the changes. Changes deep, out of sight: changes that feel like my own internal orchestration shifting. It is a strange, lightheaded experience.

In those years when I practiced yoga, for instance (poorly I must add—who is more comically stiff than an aging runner?), there were certain moments when I felt something struggling to connect, to come into being, to fuse and change. I felt it bodily. I felt it *cranially*, in some very material way inside my head. Upside down in an armstand, for example, legs scissoring in opposite directions. I laughed out loud (disturbing the solemn yoga-ness around me) because the very simple instructions "Left leg forward, right leg back" met with a woolly-headed resistance I was nearly powerless over. I watched it, this inner recalcitrance. It was like being stupid. It was funny. Week by week, month by month, I watched. Patiently I repeated the experiment, the action, and each time felt the dimwitted unwillingness of the body and the mind developing. Each time accompanied by a vaguely unmoored feeling, as if the brain were asking (slightly miffed): "So *this* is what you want now?"

I think I was changing my mind.

The same sense of inner reluctance came in playing tennis left-handed (after I destroyed my right shoulder with, what else, too much tennis). Or in getting the left hand to go along with Bach two-part inventions at an earlier stage of my keyboard adventures. When I observed my experience, it was akin to the yoga comedy: I could feel the struggle of inward change, that mild dizzy dawning inside the skull, barely but truly perceptible. I wonder if this feeling is normal.

Or to take a weightier example: sitting in the punctuated stillness of Quaker Meeting, week by week, and watching my noisy judgmental mind that wanted to silence or correct each and every speaker. I had come to silent meetings quizzically, tentatively—aware after a decade of being an ex-Christian that merely *not* being something wasn't, after all, a recipe for growth. And I needed to grow, needed to be less reactive, less judging and damaged. Yes, to let that go, to be still, to accept—that was hard. Something in me resisted and then (over time) incrementally gave way. I felt change quietly working out of sight but not quite out of the range of noticing, a faint lightheadedness. I can say that it improved me as a human. And it was funny, too, in exactly this familiar way.

What is it to live inside a brain like this? It has habits. It likes to go one familiar way. If you lead it, however, it can go another way. It can learn. Inside this learning and struggle, or this familiarity and ease, there we are. Both thinking and, you might say, being thought.

Schubert in my brain with soft tongs and velvet hammers—bending and curving, rebutting and reinforcing. He laughs as he goes. And I have to wonder, where does this lead? Who will I be when he is finished?

The Mysterious Barricades [memnoir]

This was before she started staying upstairs with sick headaches. Before sleeping in to nine o'clock, ten o'clock. Before the Valium, before the discovery of white wine. It was before I turned twelve, more or less. In those days I was used to her, of course. She kept a strictly clean and non-chaotic house, despite the three boys and the rooster husband. She deferred to him always, of course. But within her domain, we toed the line.

This is a person, I am trying to say, who awakened admiration. Whom I relied on and hoped to please, for example, by offering her little hand-sweaty bouquets picked on the long walk home from third grade, fourth, fifth. And if I got up first in the morning, I might catch her sitting at the kitchen table, gazing out toward the LA basin perhaps not smogged up yet, with her big red-edged Bible flat on the yellow Formica before her. No longer reading. Chin on hand. Motionless. If I walked down the carpeted hall quietly, I'd catch her like that. A kind of still life.

It made me wonder, *Is she sad?* She didn't look sad. She looked—something else.

That she coped at all is a wonder. Mom's family had been just herself, her mother, and her grandmother Nellie. That was it. What men she had known had disappeared. Her father, dead when she was six. Her little brother, taken in infancy. And Nellie's own absent-headed husband: there but not there since the mysterious fall. A smiling vacancy. "Best jail I was ever in," was his all-purpose quip.

Our boy-clobbered house was often invaded by neighbor boys (Tommy and Scott), sometimes by the three cousins and their dad, our father's only sibling. Without warning we could get up a small male mob for water balloons, horsing around, wrestling. Boy smells, bathroom jokes, endless throwing-things, falling-out-of-things, silliness, dumbness. The works.

Hard to imagine what she made of the scene she found herself immersed in.

≡

Mom and Dad came to hear me in my great hour. I was to read my fifth-grade essay at a school assembly, my first literary triumph (or nearly first: that I could recite two funny poems by Ogden Nash was already regarded as evidence of a significant future).

The topic was patriotic, something like "Why America Is the Best Country Ever." Maybe the prompt was more sophisticated, but that's how we took it. And I went at that topic with an unnerving certainty. I had already heard plenty in my short life about the bad and pathetic Russians and, in contradistinction, the Greatness Of America, which had according to my essay a lot to do with being able to a) *have hot showers*; b) *drive in your own car*; and c) my big closer: *Go To the SUPERMARKET!!* This was about the time that giant-sized grocery stores had appeared with vast parking lots and the marvel of self-opening doors. The boys had to be prevented from spending the entire visit jumping on the rubber mat to trigger the hissing double glass panels. Inside, it was aisles and aisles of everything and a whole rack of comic books where we could lounge on the polished linoleum floor while Mom shopped. It is easy to imagine her relief.

I took my mother shopping again just a little while ago, before leaving for Paris. The experience offered a kind of bent nostalgia. Here I am, towering over her in my balding, stiltlike way, trying to help. She is still petite, still attractive—she has been a beautiful woman for how many decades now?—but in her nineties easily flustered. My help only makes her forget what she was thinking, what she came here for. I can see this. So ... I claim to be interested in the magazine rack. "I'll just go read for a few minutes while you find what you need," is my line. I can see her relief, once again. In all these years she has never found a way to be comfortable under our gaze—ours and Dad's—our collective, judging, man-inflected way of looking at her. She couldn't hit, couldn't throw, and couldn't keep up with the banter. It left her flat and deflated. Weary, I think. (Yet with her girlfriends from church, how vivacious!)

In the school assembly, I shone brightly. She and Dad seemed to like me, they were proud. I was sure of it.

≡

The essay contest must have been a by-product of that political year: Nixon versus Kennedy. At ten years old you just absorb what your parents believe.

I heard them talking to the other grown-ups at the Baptist church. They all held that you couldn't elect a Catholic to the presidency because he would just take orders from the Pope.

But when I watched the debate on television, Kennedy did not sound the way they said—like he was trying to fool us and turn the country over to that Pope (whoever he was). And then, at some point, I heard his speech about religion and politics. Probably just a little snip played on the news. It has become famous of course, so it is hard, at this point, to sift out what part I understood then.

What I remember is a vague discomfort. I had a feeling something was not right about this way of thinking. As if my parents were bending their view of things to get around something they wouldn't name. It was exactly the same feeling I had had when my other Grandma told me not ever to put pennies or nickels in my mouth. To clinch the point, she said, "A Negro might have touched them." She had a confident, erect way of holding her head, silver hairdo always exact. We were driving somewhere. I took the coins out of my mouth. But something was wrong with what she had said. It didn't make any sense. Who cared if someone touched something? It reminded me of the way our Grandpa talked about nuns when he saw them on the street; he had bad names for them. Otherwise, he was a very sweet old guy, whiskey smell and all.

Adults had a way of talking that seemed to swerve invisibly, like something was in their way. But I didn't know what it was. Maybe they didn't either.

=

My dad and his brother had found land up in the pine-covered mountains south of Los Angeles, and they built roomy new twin cabins fifty yards apart for us to spend summers in. Better yet, Uncle Bob bought a fat, brown, black-maned Welsh pony, and stabled her right there. How lucky can a kid be? The cousin-boys named her Lassie. We all got to ride her once we had learned how to handle the tack and all.

The mountain town was in a wide granite-rimmed bowl, blue-forested on its further edges in the summer haze. I knew how to walk out our back door and continue straight up the wooded slopes, making zigs and zags to lessen the steepness, but keeping on a general bearing to hit what we called the Long Trail. It went right along our side of the valley, climbing eventually toward a pass. I had walked on the Long Trail often enough. But on this day, I was trying it on top of Lassie. And I planned to go further than ever.

I had a peanut-butter sandwich in a brown paper bag folded under my belt on one side. I wore Penney's jeans cut off at the knee, and my own invention was to leave the severed pant-legs drooping around my ankles. I believed they were thus somewhat like boots or boot tops anyway. Such as one might wear while riding. I was already a lengthy child, loosely assembled, and my legs hung down around the pony's sides. We rode bareback, with just a leather bridle and a simple bit. Of course, Lassie outweighed any of us by a huge margin, and the bit did not really equalize the contest. She turned when we told her. Provided she felt like it.

Angling this way and that through the forest, we reached the Long Trail. I dismounted and we scrambled up onto its reassuring obviousness. I turned us left, toward the pass—toward what an older boy who lived there year-round had called "the Back Country." That sounded captivating. We would walk in that direction. I climbed back up, Lassie sighed, and on we rocked. In the solitude every turn and tree, every little view or sound seemed to be my own, like a quiet possession, a satisfaction.

About the time I was thinking of my peanut butter sandwich, the trail snaked up toward a sharp turn. At that point I could see a boulder, evidently dislodged from above right onto the path. Lassie trudged up and stopped about five feet short. Pitched one of her longsuffering sighs, her flanks expanding under my legs, then contracting dolefully. The trail bent off to the right. The chunk of granite, thigh-high, just sat there in the turn. There was room to step around it.

I kicked with my tennis-shoe heels, twitched the reins. "Giddyup Lassie," I said in my bossy voice. Nothing. I repeated it. Still nothing. I looked carefully: no snake. Nothing.

I got off to pull on the reins gently, then firmly, then at a near 45-degree angle, *insisting* that she follow me around the rock. But she had decided this was it, and now she just wanted to go home and see what might be in that manger.

I climbed back up on her sweaty back, unsure what to do next. The forest was quiet in its not-quiet way. The boulder, just there. And us. Just there in the pointed firs and long-needled pines and dusty trail-smell and clear sharp air.

Big black-speckled rock on the trail. It looked like the granite that poked up through the forest floor everywhere, sometimes big solitary boulders, truck-sized, house-sized, just sitting there in the forest, like they'd been dropped off. You could climb up to sit on one, twelve feet above anybody, and be like a little vizier, a quiet lord of the domain. It would have paintlike splotches, skintight, unpeelable: gray and whitish and bright yellow-green. Also mosses, dark and crispy in our dry summers. And a litter of cones and cone bits shredded off by squirrels, plus twigs and whatnot you could flip down off the perch. And you would feel the unsmooth surface of the boulder marking your palms and your butt, like giant salt crystals. The shiny black bits we knew were called "mica" (confusingly like the book of the Bible), because someone had once showed us a wide smoky-transparent wafering of it in a hunk of split-open granite, like the inside of a piece of weird fruit. Mica.

I looked down at the obstructing rock, just a small cousin of the big boulders. I felt, if anything, friendly toward it.

But mostly I felt the forest itself, which often seemed almost to be sighing, a sound high up in the tall tops that you might also feel passing on the soft of your cheek. It was just there, all around us. Like the beards of lime-green lichen dangling from limbs and trunks and creeping even out onto twigs and falling on the floor with the deadwood litter. It grew, it fell, it was just there. Where we were.

But what did it mean, after all? Lassie, the refusal, the boulder and the quick turn and the long new trail that stretched onward to . . . well, it could be infinity for all I knew. I wasn't frightened, not by the what-was-lurking aspect. Though it was a little eerie. The silent moment.

There was no forest-fear. The forest was familiar to me. I played in it every day. It nodded in the windows of our sleeping loft, and we escaped down its branches sometimes, out the window on the back side away from the doors, to walk around and have night adventures. There were certain tall trees we climbed to get to the very highest rungs where the trunk would, amazingly, have become slim enough to get our arms all the way around, to ride it back . . . and forth . . . across the shocking distance those treetops travelled even in a light breeze. The trees left pitch on your arms and your T-shirt and your jeans. That was all.

What I felt wasn't fear. It was a sense I had no words for. An odd calm. An unreadable presence.

After standing there in the not-silent silence for a while, Lassie sighed, turned around, and headed us for home.

A remembered evening, soon after, makes a strange twin to that moment in the forest—also silent, also overflowing. They are locked together in my mind.

Most summer nights we stayed outside playing after dinner all the way to nightfall, which came late. Mom could make a piercing whistle with two fingers in the sides of the mouth like a cowboy or a coach, loud enough to summon us from blocks away. We were trained to come, *now*, when we heard it. Or else.

We had been playing hide and seek, all six of the brothers and cousin-boys. It felt exotic and wild to be playing so long and so late, there among the tall rough-barked trees, and we'd run like crazy after being discovered, flying for no reason in the dim light and the darkness and the warm air loaded up with vanilla-scent from the Ponderosa pines. She whistled and I came back to her first, by myself. I let myself in quietly, my head full of the fragrant dusk and the spin and hush of it all. And there in the big open room of the cabin she stood in semidarkness, looking out the window. Her hair was reddish that summer but in the twilight just dark and full, banded across the top but falling free toward her shoulders. A rim of violet sky shone through the window from above the outline of dark pine tops. There was a kind of glow coming in. And her standing motionless at the window.

As if in amber, that moment. I don't mean love or sentiment or gratitude. Those are good things, but they are not what I mean. It was the way my mother stood, silently, in that side-lighted gloaming. In her beauty.

What I mean is her *strangeness.*

Who was this person, after all? She was like the forest. I felt them both. I knew them, relied on them, trusted them. I loved them both, I knew that. In different ways. But they were so strange.

And what, after all, had they to do with me?

Vermeer and Rembrandt

Coming of age in the mid-twentieth century somewhere between Kennedy and Nixon—those opposing versions of presidential machismo—I recall vividly that Rembrandt occupied a unique position. He was the cultural token that meant capital-A Art: high culture, profundity, Old Masters, the works. Rembrandt was the bust in the niche, familiar even to the unschooled. A Rembrandt image was as likely to appear on a cigar box or a Red Skelton television skit as in an art history lecture.

But now, some fifty years later, as I come belatedly to my maturity as an art viewer, I find the bust has been switched out. No one talks about Rembrandt like that any more; he has lost out to Vermeer. One Dutchman for another, but what a world of difference.

"What is it about Vermeer?" asks Peter Schjeldahl, whose precise and unpretentious writing about visual art is its own kind of wonder for me these days. "Everyone idolizes him . . . he's a trend!" Vermeer is suddenly as ubiquitous as *The Night Watch* once was. It's hard to know what to make of it, this popularity, this shimmer and buzz suddenly shared by so many. His *Girl with a Pearl Earring* became a novel and then a movie with big stars. You can get a children's book about Vermeer. There's a documentary. Even an opera.

And I'm as besotted as anyone. For Vermeer I would travel—*have* traveled. Any one of the precious thirty-five canvases is, for me, a potential breakthrough, a story told to my inmost self. A Vermeer promises an experience of a certain irreplaceable kind—that blaze of feeling and somehow undisclosed import. Like the first time I heard Beethoven's Ninth performed live, at nineteen years old. Or the Emerson Quartet, just after the millennium. My first Tom Stoppard play. Ai Wei Wei at the Venice Biennale.

Above all there's my Vermeer Moment, which I usually hold back talking about. It's that important in my little story, my private pilgrimage.

Of course, Rembrandt is still venerated, still secure in art history. Of course, one walks observantly through his rooms at the Louvre. Dutifully.

Yes, yes . . . but Vermeer fascinates. His paintings are few and glisteningly still. Something is being wrestled with in those painted chambers of young women, golden light, and suspended time. There's a question hovering there, a shimmer of possibility we all recognize though probably cannot name. These canvases seem to offer a glimpse into the essential mystery: *our* mystery, *our* sense of possibility. As Rembrandt was the contemporary of the feeling intellect of the 1950s and '60s, it seems to me that Vermeer has become our contemporary, now, today.

Vermeer has become—to use Schjeldahl's word—*necessary*.

≕

A few years ago, I was offered an apartment in Amsterdam for six weeks, courtesy of an absent musician friend who had purchased the flat for his occasional European gigs. So my partner and I came to bask in the busy city, the nearby towns and countryside, the churches and museums. And to do it all without hurry.

Best of all was the Amsterdam museum pass granting us unlimited entry. We sampled other museums, but soon the Rijksmuseum became my hangout, my almost-daily stroll. It's a huge collection, of course, with overpowering riches in the Old Masters. And everyone who has travelled knows the frustration of dashing through collections like this, seeing too much and absorbing too little, with aching feet and swimming head. Here was my antidote: leisure. Repetition. Selectivity. The luxury of seeking out, sometimes, just that one painting to re-see, to contemplate. And on the way out, merely looking around randomly. Sampling, tasting. And leaving.

This was before the Rijksmuseum received its glitzy makeover. It was then a staid old pile, vast and dowagerlike. Daily I entered the broad passageway where the building arched to allow pedestrians to cross under. It marked the arrival of my twenty-minute walk, where Russian buskers with accordions stood to play Bach fugues, precise and resonant. Always a euro for them. Always a pause, a flight of mind and heart and moment. And then I was ready to go in.

By the second week my partner and I had already settled into a pattern. Once inside we liked to separate, each to his own exploration, then rejoin after a couple hours to compare notes, perhaps backtrack and share what was discovered. My partner is an artist; I'm a writer. We can go hammer-and-tongs disagreeing over one piece, then suddenly coincide over the next.

I have learned to take my own opinions with a grain of salt. And not to get too melodramatic with the reasons.

So it was with a suppressed intensity that I found myself staring at Vermeer's *Milkmaid*. It was midweek, the halls were quiet, the rooms calm. And as I looked, something welled up in me. Oh, yes, everyone loves this painting, and I'm everyone, nothing special about me. There she stood. The gentle intensity of light from the left, that mullion'd window. The sturdy girl, girt about for her workday, standing in a lucid glow as she holds up a pouring pitcher. The blue of her apron, the gold of the light. Her head inclined, poised, steady in the work, which is neither rushed nor delayed. Her expression placid, attentive.

Just a painting. Yet . . . a kind of universe. Inexpressible.

Later that morning, my partner and I returned there together, and side by side we kept silence, looking. I had decided not to advertise my emotions. Just let the thing be. Tears, though, were under my eyelids, and a sense of the indwelling mystery of everything I had ever loved: the far peaks I had climbed to get pure light and solitude; the way I had toiled in my library carrel all those years to find something knowable and true; the way music eluded and carried and blessed and disappeared. The way love came. All of it, too much to talk about. So I didn't. Then his voice from beside me, muted and calm: "Kind of makes you want to cry, doesn't it?" He's braver about emotion than I am. And he was having, all unprompted, the exact same experience. Vermeer was at the center of something. He was the necessity of art. He was proof and warrant of this life of wandering and looking. Vermeer.

Over Amsterdam coffee and sweets we laughed at our synchronicity. Gingerly we tried words to get at the mystery of it: that mystery we had both staked our lives upon, the faith that in words or images *something can happen that changes the world*. A very little change, perhaps. But real—however difficult to put words to, in any satisfactory way.

In time we found the other Vermeers that Holland had to offer. Then we saw those in the Louvre and at the Met and the Frick on our return through New York, ending up with a tidy little tally of Vermeers. Not every one tipped us into ecstasy, not by far. Some of his girls have rather silly faces, I think, with a kind of cowlike blandness. And there's an allegorical dame that is a laugh-out-loud failure. But many had exactly what had shaken us so with *The Milkmaid*: Stillness. Light. Humanity. Intimacy. Tenderness.

But why? Why this turn toward Vermeer over the last decade or two? It's a history-of-ideas kind of question that can lead to facile generalization. How would anyone measure such a thing, this shared idea, this trend, this feeling that moves through a population so mysteriously? Does it even exist?

We feel it. Then we try to explain it. Here's my best shot.

There's a muscularity in Rembrandt. With his darks and lights and his command of the moment, the subject seems *subjected* to the painter. Rembrandt is about mastery. Each canvas is a bravura performance of strength, the dark power of technique and confidence. Rembrandt is a man's man.

Whose man is Vermeer? No one's. Vermeer leaves a feeling of his absence. As Schjeldahl remarks, it is as if he has just left the scene. Instead he gives himself to the canvas, the light, the moment—most of all to his women, women who are his subjects almost exclusively. There may be a man in the frame as letter bearer, music teacher, drinking partner. But the focus (with just three exceptions) is always the woman.

Whereas Rembrandt, by a wide margin (perhaps three to one), paints mostly men. Certainly his most renowned subjects are men: *The Night Watch*, *The Anatomy Lesson*, the many self-portraits. These men stand forth from the darkness, for it seems darkness is the native element of Rembrandt's painted world, and only by force of will does the figure emerge into the light. Even in a group pose, and certainly in the many gentlemanly portraits, each man feels aloof, spotlighted, a solitary (if temporary) victor. It feels like the drama of individualism.

Strength, control, and individualism: those are certainly the manly values I grew up with—that I strived for, fell short of (shamefully), or occasionally reached—the very nub of what my life seemed meant to mean. While I found this struggle grueling, as it must have been for many other men and boys of the 1950s and early 60s, it was nonetheless an almost unchallenged cultural standard. Weakness was not to be displayed or admitted. We men needed to *take* our place, and the challenge demanded everything of us.

And Vermeer? In his world the light is given, not taken. The women he depicts inhabit the moment; they don't strain or grasp. Their world is flooded with beauty, instinct with meaning. And wholly available, though entirely mute—hovering within the instant, yet impossible to possess or even understand.

For whatever reason, we are drawn there now. Those strivers of Rembrandt, those men of arms and wealth, have come to seem more like the unfortunate backdrop of life—reckless and destructive—not its goal. For that, we look elsewhere. And Vermeer promises us: if you look, it will be waiting for you.

—

And so this year Paris offers me another chance at Vermeer. I can return to the Louvre as often as I like and in the off-season too. It was ten, no twelve years ago we lingered in Amsterdam. Now we are slower of foot but still willing. And yes, there are the Vermeers, without ceremony: second floor, Richelieu wing, northwest corner. *The Astronomer*, with its sad footnote of Nazi history. And *The Lace-Maker*, poised, perfect. Just these two, amid the hoarded excess of this museum. Just two.

What is it we seek? Sometimes it is found here. Or sometimes discovered in a different room. Or on the walk home, lost in contemplation, lost in the crowd, when the light of latest afternoon slants under the gray lid of winter, crossing us with glory. And we find ourselves not heroic individualists who have conquered Paris or Life or anything. No. We are simply blessed—blessed by breath or by consciousness . . . or by what, exactly? By that briefest mystery, mere being and awareness. Shared mutely with so many others on the moiling boulevards of the metropolis.

Vasty Love and the Big Comedown [memnoir]

The night before my departure from the secret valley above Goddard Canyon, that cut-off land in the sky with no trails where I spent a week on my own, just me and the Jeff pines and the trout, I took a midnight walk up to where I remembered a place of particular clarity. I had noticed it a week earlier, on the way down from the ridge. This was the night of the new moon, which means of course *no* moon. Even so, such walking is better without a flashlight. Seeing adjusts in due time to the gray-silver eye scale of the night, and soon the Milky Way strewn overhead provides light, light, plenty of light. If you know your way and walk that way.

When I got there it was as I recalled: a perfectly Sierran place, emblematic, where wide benches of polished and bedrocky granite stepped down and paused at each stage, and the coming-down streamlet made little splashy cascades and brooks that lingered in tarns among the short mossy meadow-grass, the deepblue gentians black in starlight, the shrub and open rock. We could look down and see the forest below, dark, resting or not-resting. "We" means *me* in company with the place toward which I felt a companionship. That was how I did it in those days.

Above me: that universe.

I had brought my down sleeping bag as a comforter, to drape over my shoulders and thighs against the cold air descending from the heights, as I regarded it all and tilted my head back to look up and tried to keep a matching silence. I have stared into this sky how many thousands of times? It was my friend on mountain treks and desert treks too. In fact, I planned for it, bringing star charts and a strange old book of sidereal names and etymologies: Rasalhague, Aldeberan, Zaidec, Algenubi, Persian Greek Latin Arabic sounds mouth-filling and mind-filling enough to match even this overspread of excess, this abundance. There I am, solitary, silhouette peaks ridged all around. Close by are the sighs and points of the stunted pines of ten thousand feet. Closer still the mirror-pool of stars impounded at my feet, oceaned overhead.

And I am dizzy with all sublime, all colossal, all impossible. For how many years has it been my best teacher? That one inaudible perennial that said:

All this :: All this :: Breathe :: Breathe :: Breathe

And this moment was mine, absorbed, a silent nutrient of the spirit.

Even as a certain loneliness made itself felt—a sense of needing to go back. This disturbed me. It made sense in a general way, I could see that. Who wouldn't feel it? Yet it was a surprise.

═

I caught a few hours of sleep back in my encampment, but at first light I awoke and got myself walking up the not-trail trail, my old green pitch-stained Kelty backpack fully loaded but lighter by a week of eaten-up noodles and tuna and bulgur and fig bars. I felt strong, eager. The way was known, I could see it clearly in my mind's eye, I would be up in the notch before noon and take my lunch on the other side. And have stories to tell when I got back.

Can I say that I felt, like, righteous? In the surfer-lingo sense. I felt squared away or as Hemingway's beautifully manly character Brett would say, *set up.* Yes, ready, fulfilled, and as long as no one was around to play humble for, rather proud of myself. Months and months earlier, I had begun augmenting my conditioning beach runs with hikes around my neighborhood, after classes were taught and papers set aside to be marked after dinner. I carried my idiotic knapsack full of barbell weights—forty pounds of clanking up and down and back up the wee hills of Mar Vista—to get the legs ready and to push back against the softness of forty. Push back hard.

And here was the payoff earned by perseverance, by two summers of recon trips, by fortitude and, maybe, a little, by courage. Oh yes, I was a clean-faced brisk-walking up-we-go fellow. At mid-morning I had already gained back half the elevation, and so I stopped for a snack and a quick rest. Eyeing that notch, still small and far and buried in morning shadow.

Can you see, brother reader, sister reader, what must come next? In retrospect it is inevitable, the irony demanded by the cosmic storyteller. First came the broken tooth. As I munched a granola bar and gazed downvalley in mid-morning euphoria, *snap* it went. I, who had been turning the earth with my legs, striding upward with the gods, *snap* it went. An upper tooth, half way back on the right. I felt with my tongue in that panicked way, *oh god how bad is it,* and then with my finger. No blood. Just a sharp-edged stump. *Damn.* Pause for recollecting. *Well no harm really; just chew on the other side for the remainder. Soon it'll be all downhill, make a lot of mileage, three days to get in but just two to get out . . .*

About that time another ache began to intrude into my resting moment. It came from the other direction. It was down there in the rearward precincts. Where, as a fine fit fortysomething, I had never had any kind of trouble. Though I had heard of it.

Wasn't this swelling extrusion something for, like, pregnant ladies? Certainly not for a fellow like me. Certainly not this nasty, unclean thing. *Good god, what is happening to me?*

The light came up and came up, the shadows shrank and the warmth came, ah, golden in the morning, but I was not relishing not basking not glowing no not one bit. I was aching, worrying about how this *thing* would be to climb with, how it would feel under this damned heavy backpack and thirty miles to get out of here. Oh nasty, oh *faugh,* oh *damn.*

———

What I thought was my life, was not my life. Or not the whole of it. I wish I could say I'm talking about the mild comedy of trail mishaps. But that was mere foretaste, a light preparatory tap from the perverse reality that really wants pratfalls and the harder the better. (Reality is quite vulgar, it seems.) If you think yourself happy, get ready to think again.

This is a hard thing to accept when you're all mountainy and strong. Or, equally, when you're back in your daily life down in the flats, in your dowdy car and second-rate college, teaching your inattentive students and yet feeling that you're not doing so bad, no, you're still in the profession after all, while so many of your grad-school cohort have given up and moved on to selling real estate or whatever. Here you still are. Your first book is published at last. Your stupid job has allowed you a bourgeois foothold, a tiny stucco two-bedroom bungalow of your own, just a quick two-mile drive down Venice Boulevard to morning beach runs. And sunset beach walks, hand in hand with the other prized achievement. The beloved.

To be solid and loved at forty! At last! Way to go!

When I finally arrived back to Culver City, the youngish man in question had seemed strangely distant. I see that now. My car was still ticking hot in the driveway as I stood in our little 1950s kitchen trying to unload my excitement to him, how hard it had been but easy really, beautiful really, perfect really. He was strangely disengaged. Eventually I gathered that he wasn't going to react, so I just shrugged and filed it away to think about later. Went to unpack the car. Take a shower. See about our dinner.

He had been my partner for nine years. It was a stretch of happiness and contentment I had believed could never come to me, the long-delayed retort to the miseries of my churchy, god-damaged upbringing. I felt right in my life. Brisk. Squared away. Set-up.

The unreadable strangeness of other people—I had always taken it as a glitch. A frustration and an annoyance. To combat it, I always made a point of saying exactly what I meant, no coy subtexts or unacknowledged agendas. And that meant always knowing, for myself, exactly what I did want. What I intended. It was for clarity, a kind of hygiene, to avoid scenes and mistakes. Probably it was part of my early self-discipline, keeping myself safe and monitored and unsullied while I prayed over my inner dirtiness.

But of course these notions did not assist me in my dealings with the humans, whom I found continuously oblique and self-contradictory. Even the handsome ones that I lived with for so long and in such joy.

I have come to a different sense, all these years later. I think that in this incomprehensibility is something both darker and grander. It is a kind of event horizon within each of us, a boundary marking that which is inexpressible. It is, in its darkness, that least-loved kind of sublimity—that chaos, that bewilderer, that mad destroyer of dreams and cozy delusions. That lightless place where we, ourselves, are formless and unknown.

Perhaps it is this darkness that makes love (when it happens) the even-stranger miracle. That love *is* at all, I mean to say, against this dense and unseeable core around which we spin, self unknown, other unknown. The unknowability is not a glitch. It is the wild *thisness* that brings time and space and personality and life into existence, all around itself.

I would not want to pretend that thinking about sublimity and darkness and so forth will get me out of the catastrophe of life, the suffering and pain and dislocation that flood in upon us until there's nothing to be done but endure. There is no transcending it. Emptiness and abandonment do unspeakable things to us, out of scale and without meaning. And we walk as if bloody footed, struggling to go on.

He was kind to me as we separated. He held me as I wept, saying: *Breathe. Breathe.*

I learned something about how fragile people may be, and how little strength might be left us. How you might think—probably truthfully—*one more like this and I'm done for.* How I became more tender to others. This was something important. It dawned on me slowly, over the years of slogging forward, as I moved to my new town of Portland, wangled a new job, lived in a new old house. I found a simplicity. I got down off my high horse. I came to know that a touch, a look, a kindness could be more precious than any striving for distant grandeur. I accepted without shame—at last!—that I was needy and sometimes meager. Just like everyone else.

But I can also say that there were provisions available when all else seemed taken away. The mountains had built a silence within me that was tough and deep. Years and years, alone and alone. The stars had already taught me that I was a smallness—and now undoubtedly so, yes, painfully proven. It is true that as I dealt with loneliness and loss, I often felt diminished almost to extinction. It was frightening to be on this brink, standing with my toes over such emptiness. It hurt. Sometimes it seemed like old pain from my terrorized youth, when God himself threatened.

But I had also learned this: that I was a smallness with a largeness built inside it. The starry void was within me too. It was beautiful, capacious, and despite everything it made me feel strangely worthy. There was a vast quiet of great beauty, inhuman and yet beckoning. This was not comfort, exactly. It was not an answer to life's unsolvables. But it was something to go forward on. I went forward.

The Northwest gave me riches. I found a grove of oldest trees, and I went there often. I sat by powerful rivers and watched them change, motion and light, hours and hours.

=

I write this in the pearly light of an early Paris morning, stirred by memory. The Pantheon glimmers a half-mile away; the opportunities of Paris lie all around us. But on his cot in the corner my partner dozes, and his breathing offers a softness that fills this quiet, otherwise impersonal place, this studio that is ours for a short while. He feels close and real. We have shared this adventure, he on his path and I on mine. The studio is his, of course, since the residency is his. Here he makes art. I just have a little table over on the side that I use as a desk, and we fold it up out of the way when it's time for studio visits and expositions.

Such a strange coda to all that climbing and losing, that low comedy of tears and damage and exile!

He sleeps while I work, but I breathe his air. He is my life's great second chance, a better sequel than I could have imagined. I have no more great climbs left in my legs. It took me years to find him, and now, still more years along, we are solid and right. He is a blessing.

All the nobility of mountains and all the straining pomp of Paris cannot speak to the way love needs a place of ordinary habitation. Love and pain are the grounded realities, earthbound. They are the ache of flesh that frames our limits: for while we stare in raptures at the stars, our feet begin to get cold. And then we go indoors where someone beloved will wrap us in arms or laugh at our wild eyes and make us chop onions for dinner.

In all the universe around us, is there a paradox to match this: that we love so near, and desire so distant and grand?

At this moment, this morning, I am unsure how to resolve the paradox of connectedness, how to place love within the grandeurs of the sublime. For within the near precincts of the heart, love too is a galaxy, rich and impossible to measure. It speaks our nighest name, and when we hear it, we know ourselves strangely. As if in some new world.

Breakable, yes. Disappointing. Occasionally meager. Yet, from time to time, filled to overflowing with something we cannot even name.

Umpteenth Brumaire

My life has taught me that, at certain moments, we can think beyond our cultural conditioning, be surprised by a word that breaks through. I look for this transcendence. I welcome it and nourish it. I have a sense of my own biography as a record of such moments, when I have been rescued—saved perhaps—by a stroke of beauty, connectedness, truth.

Yes, nature can speak to us; so can the deep wells of being itself. The arts can be conduits for it, as can simple acts of love and compassion.

But we must not kid ourselves about where we live the rest of the time. In the broad light and clashing sound of day, we are indeed back inside our own skins, burdened by history and trudging along exactly as anyone would predict. Transcending nothing.

History comes around like the mailman, like herpes, like the five-second laugh-track cycle on a sitcom. After a certain age—I reached it long ago—there's a sort of dreadful familiarity to the unfolding: Here we go again. A scandal. A bubble. A swindle. A war. The news media go along with the joke, the unthinkable becomes policy, and we look at each other mutely—we citizens, we subjects, we dupes and consumers—with our eyebrows raised. For an instant, a single thought balloon materializes above our briefly collective heads: *Surely not.* We mistrust our ears, our eyes. *What th'* . . . ?

History repeats itself until it becomes an inane mumble, no longer intelligible.

As I write, the hacks and profiteers who orchestrated our country's Iraq debacle are attaching themselves to the various Republican presidential candidates queuing up for the first post-Obama election. They are making the same old noises. *War. War. War alone can save us.* I suppose it will be a chance to measure the length of the public memory. Will these inexhaustible has-beens be allowed to rewrite history under the noses of those who actually lived it, as Hannah Arendt quipped? Will we believe their interestingly fictive account of our own recent experience?

Karl Marx famously says that when history repeats itself, the first time is tragedy, but the second is farce. It's a nifty observation, hilarious and angry. Just reading it relieves some of my bewilderment. Yes. Exactly.

But no one is laughing. Tragedy, farce . . . then what? What to call the third time? The fourth or the fortieth? I need a better language. Truer. Or angrier. Or something. I don't know what show I'm watching.

≡

In Paris you live with history. This is a truism, but for a boy from the thin and recent habitations of the far West, it is also a palpable shock each time I come here. The casual presence of the past, as life goes on in its bones, in its marrow. So is it actually even past? I don't think we know about this in Portland, Seattle, Bakersfield, LA. We think the past is something in a book. We see ourselves living in a sort of continuous present, bright with opportunity like oranges ready to be plucked. And our ravaged forests can still make you believe they're virgin.

But here is Notre Dame in my window, a few minutes' walk downriver. I watch its carved towers and slate roof turn gray-shiny in the winter wet. The shower passes, and on my way to the Latin Quarter I go striding by the stone towers of the Conciergerie, that ancient scene of state torture. But next door at the Palace of Justice, fresh-pressed uniforms stand guard with automatic weapons, the quintessence of the moment. Everywhere I pass old buildings built around even older ones, housing the utterly new—Apple stores, fashionable boutiques—like bright dragonflies newly alighted.

For my late-morning indulgence of reading and sentence making, I stop at a favored coffee bar. A furred and overdressed older Parisienne sits dourly beside intense young students from the Sorbonne and the University of Paris, founded by Abelard—*Abelard!*—who rallied his students in that very alley, just over there. Week by week I come here to sip and read the news, alternating *Le Monde* with the *New York Times*. President Sarkozy gone. Gone his retro capitalism and his hated austerity policies borrowed from the Germans and the English. Dancing in the streets for his replacement François Hollande. Think of it—a leftist—a Socialist!

Who almost immediately rolls out a pallid version of . . . more austerity.

≡

Here's the money quote from Marx, the opening salvo in his essay "The Eighteenth Brumaire of Louis Napoleon," a laughing-despairing lampoon of the French politics of the 1840s and '50s, which had culminated in, of all things, a brand-new Napoleonic monarch:

> Hegel remarks somewhere that all great, world-historical facts and personages occur, as it were, twice. He has forgotten to add: the first time as tragedy, the second time as farce.

Napoleon Bonaparte's nephew was a man of excellent whisker. On December 2, 1851, a cabal both rich and decorated (like pastry) made him Emperor. He looked the part. It was a coup of the late fall, mirroring his uncle's 1799 coup in the month that had been renamed "Brumaire" (foggy) by blissed-out revolutionaries who believed they had begun the world anew, at the Year Zero. Only to find, of course, that it was still the same old world, ready to fall for cocked hats and strutting patriots. And so in the fullness of time came another Brumaire, another Napoleon—this one without even talent to recommend him. Instead he had the wealthy; or they had him.

The farce had begun three years earlier with this very Louis Bonaparte being elected president. A startling political fervor had arisen to replace the tired-out monarch Louis-Philippe. The Second Republic churned its inwards, half the peasantry and all the bourgeoisie coalesced around this lump, and with a kind of excremental inevitability Louis Bonaparte became *Monsieur le Président*, a gentleman for the times—which meant, for business. In due time he cooled into a sort of *M. l'Empereur*.

What followed the presidential/imperial coup, when it finally came forth, was the usual smutty clean up. A few hundred killed in the streets. Thousands imprisoned. Penal colonies in Algeria. Censorship, repression. A gilded grip, making everything better for one's betters. Victor Hugo and many others in voluntary exile. But under the reassuring gaze of a Napoleon (any Napoleon!) an air of pious moneymaking soon cloaked all unpleasantness.

The Paris that I live in, it is largely his Paris. M. l'Empereur hired Baron von Haussmann to remodel the old wiggly-streeted *ville*, with results that all the world admires. And at the heart of the broad new avenues he placed the perfect Napoleonic confection: the Paris Opera (Opéra Garnier). Indescribable, indigestible, gilded and chandeliered and curlicued beyond taste, beyond reason, beyond imagining, all to prove the regime's success, respectability, *bah oui*, legitimacy. To see it is a master course in the intimate relation of kitsch and governance.

That was a farce for the ages. We're buying tickets still.

═══

But what shall we feel, how shall we applaud, when farce (or one of its suc-
cessor genres) sweeps away all that is realest and hardest won in the com-
monwealth of citizenship and liberty? Marx watched in horror as Napoleon
III, aping the original Revolution yet mistaking it in every detail, demolished
democracy. He wrote: *What seems overthrown is no longer the monarchy; it is
the liberal concessions that were wrung from it by century-long struggles.*

We imagine a thing solid because it has stood for a few generations.
We are creatures of the year, or perhaps the decade. But then, an *entire
people suddenly finds itself set back into a dead epoch.* Hasn't this happened
recently, to you, to me? Weirdly outmoded language suddenly heard again,
orotund and empty: *homeland*, Divine blessing. Pick your decade, pick your
war: Iraq, Guatemala, Grenada, Vietnam in its sixth, eighth, tenth year. Pick
your bubble, your collapse, your claque of thieving financiers and complicit
politicians: savings and loan scandal, Great Railway Bubble, dot-com bust,
Great Depression, Great Recession.

It has taken me a few days to think this through. Now I sit in a café
on rue du Temple, in the third arrondissement, remembering the American
election of November 2000 and all that followed. Did anyone really foresee
that *torture* would become public policy, defended in broad daylight by banal
men with elevated titles? Did anyone foresee that *public education*, the consensus project of a century and a half, would become a partisan target—to
be scorned, subverted, defunded, privatized? Or that the *right to vote* itself,
as exercised by the poor and the not-white, should be abridged just a few
decades after it was won? Even as Martin Luther King's monstrous statue
entombs his memory on the National Mall and is vacantly praised by the
very same malefactors.

Or that Great Recession bailouts would offer the largest single wealth
transfer (straight upward, of course) in the history of the planet—aided,
about equally, by members of both parties?

Or could any of Obama's progressive partisans (myself included) have
foreseen that the much-feared black president—champion of the poor,
bringer of health care—would adopt a rightist Heritage Foundation scheme
to turn the entire health-care project over to insurance companies, which
have embarked on a festival of self-enrichment worthy of the Gilded Age?

When I read Marx's *Eighteenth Brumaire*, how immediate it feels. It
could have been written today, this very afternoon. I could have bought it a

coffee, and we could have sat quietly working on our two sides of the little table. And if I had dared to peep out from under the Napoleonic cloak of bourgeois manners, to suggest (however timidly) restraint, amelioration, oh the canting arguments, the horrified objections that would rain down on us! *Every demand of the most ordinary liberalism, of the most formal republicanism, of the most insipid democracy, is simultaneously castigated as an "attempt on society" and stigmatised as "socialism."*

And it dawns on me with a sort of blinking surprise, as if I were the dumbest student in the room: Has it always been like this? Really?

Why has it taken me so long to realize it?

We've been through it dozens of times, scores, hundreds, who knows? No way to keep track. For the umpteenth time, we hear the panicked cries: Our Money is at risk! Our System threatened! Fight, suffer, retrench, keep silent, give all for the Homeland! (But ask no sacrifices from plutocrats. That would be class warfare, which we cannot afford.)

We have long since had both the tragedy and the farce. So then what? What comes next in the March of Bathos?

Each time now is the umpteenth time. Uncountable. Unaccountable. Oh for another Marx brother to help us figure it out yet again. Horse feathers everywhere, another night at the Opéra. The Umpteenth Brumaire. What else to call it?

(How about: The human condition?)

Sehnsucht and the Deep Present [memnoir]

When I was sixteen, I stopped myself from reading science fiction. I had belonged to a book club—a new book every other week—and this reading was wonderfully wild and imaginative. But I wanted to begin my adult mental life, my earnest and (of course) Christian maturity. And in the New Testament St. Paul had said we must "give up childish things." I wondered what my serious reading should be.

But a woman in our Baptist church told me about an English writer, C. S. Lewis (an Oxford don—the very standard of seriousness), who had written Christian science fiction! Soon I had plodded through his three rather grim adult semi-sci-fi novels and all seven of his marvelous Narnia books for children. Then, determined, I began his nonfiction books on faith, theology, humanity, and there I encountered the word *Sehnsucht*. The learned Lewis had somehow attached this bit of German Romanticism to his evangelicalism. For me it was like strong drink.

Sehnsucht seemed like a word from a different world. It meant "longing," but carried an extra charge, a secret intensity that made it truer. Los Angeles surrounded me. I watched football with my brothers. I did what others my age did. But inwardly I was a chaos: the gay kid in the Baptist pew, the one God hated with an appalling specificity. All the predictable loneliness, the burden of self-loathing. And yet deeper than this artificially induced crisis, I felt a nameless longing. Now it had a name, Sehnsucht. Its foreignness was a kind of promise: yes, this other world exists somewhere.

≡

In Paris I make a new friend: Johanna, a poet and painter from Düsseldorf. At some point, talking of this and that, I begin trying to convey this story to her—the lure of a single word from her language, Sehnsucht. It points to strange connections between us, so we start sharing work. I brush off my German dictionary and translate her poem, "Blau ist ein Lockvogel": *Blue is a decoy.*

Blue loosens
toward the seventh heaven.
Blue is an in-between, an aperitif,
sensitive, off-center, satin.
A hint that won't stay put.

Blue finishes an adagio with weightlessness.

Blue is a decoy, a lure.
The stroke of a quill is all it takes . . .

Her poem speaks my language. So I continue the looping, indirect account: trying to explain my life of Sehnsucht amid the aridity of my childhood home in suburban Los Angeles.

In my ninth grade drama class there were sometimes unfilled hours when others were rehearsing. Rummaging in the tiny control room behind the stage, I found a set of vinyl recordings of the great harpsichordist Wanda Landowska. Secluded behind a soundproof door, I put the headphones on, doubling the hush. I laid the needle onto the turning disk. And began to absorb this music that seemed to belong to another world, ecstatic and disciplined, complicated, striving, delaying, arriving. I didn't know German but I read the words "Wohl-Tempierte Klavier" from the record jacket. On days scattered across several months, I heard all forty-eight preludes and fugues. Heard them again and again.

I had already been finding my way to Bach, for in my early teens I had taken it into my head to seek out pipe-organ music. My father was a man of business, a solid Republican with no imagination whatever, yet he delivered me without complaint down the freeways and traffic-choked boulevards to moments of impossible beauty. What he thought of his odd son is hard to guess.

Once, the cathedral organist of Notre Dame, Paris, came on a tour to Pasadena, where there was a powerful sixty-rank instrument. Pierre Cochereau thundered, he whispered, he played the Bach C-minor Passacaglia and its great fugue, electrifying me. Then he finished with the César Franck crowd-pleaser "Pièce Héroïque." This French music was strange, unhinged, wandering and yearning. It lifted me out of my known life.

⸻

Sehnsucht led me on like a talisman.

Almost anything German might carry the glow of it. Bach, of course, an ocean unto himself. And I hoped that learning a little German might open the way, so I took language courses, one year after another (though alas, there was no Sehnsucht in struggling with the dative endings). And then came Wagner. In my junior year of high school, the New York Metropolitan Opera came to town with a mighty *Das Rheingold,* performed in the hugeness of the Shrine Auditorium downtown. Far back in the balcony I sat, a lone pilgrim from the suburbs.

What fate for a teenager who comes, solitary, to listen to the story of the Ring without the slightest preparation? Oh naive and foolish! The curtain went up: green light, underwater maidens, singing, singing. Singing. Singing singing singing singing.

After an hour, I sat slumped in my seat. After two, I sank lower. Dogged, I waited it out. Singing singing singing singing. Two hours more and I was dumbstruck, bewildered, drowned. Sehnsucht appeared now and then, in moments of instrumental gorgeousness. Then it swam away out of sight.

The Wagner experiment was not a success, but I was undeterred. My ignorance would not defeat me. Had not St. Paul said that the life of the spirit was like a distance race? And wasn't I, in fact, a distance runner, thin as a whippet, long legged and untiring? I never gave up. I won my races. I acted like a correct boy, trying to imitate those I saw around me and, wherever possible, best them. But my inner goals were otherwise.

⸻

In Paris, Johanna recounts how, in her own growing up, she too found her way to Bach. Later she wrote it to me in a letter:

> Bach's music carried me through my severe respiratory disease
> even when I was still a child. . . . I discovered that while I was
> listening the constriction in my bronchia was a little easier to
> bear. In Bach I had discovered something which ever since I
> have been searching for everywhere in the arts. Something that
> stands out from the breakneck acceleration in all areas . . . the
> pressures . . . the impositions . . . the news full of catastrophes.

Listening to Bach gives me structure. Gives me the splendor of beginning, even when going astray.

It all feels eerily familiar. In those long-ago years, I wonder if we might have been listening at exactly the same moment, sometimes? A half-planet apart, were we not citizens of the same invisible place, dwellers in a solidarity of Sehnsucht? An unseen global fellowship of aspiration, readiness, the ache of the sublime. Perhaps there were others. Many others.

I have tried calling this place we belonged to *the deep present*.

≡

In LA there were more adventures. A new museum opened nearby, containing a collection of modernist paintings mysteriously called *Der Blaue Reiter*. Why "blue"? Where were they riding? I was stricken with wonder. Kandinsky. Klee. The colors saturated, delicious, alien. I was ignorance itself, and no one in my life ever talked about anything like this. But there it was before my eyes.

This was in the Norton Simon Museum, the *noblesse-oblige* residue of an industrialist's life of power seeking, money seeking. Strange, isn't it. Upstairs I saw a still life by Zurbarán that riveted me. I still go to look at it when I return to Los Angeles. A bowl of lemons. A cup. A small pink rose.

But what these meant I could not say.

≡

It was on my first night in Salzburg that the connection finally clicked. I was twenty, on a three-month "study tour" with too many other American students, plus three profs who nightly tried to fill our empty heads.

I had walked out alone. Here was our *pension*, on a cobbled street. A block away was a church where Mozart had played. Mozart! And nearby, along this street: a tavern, a laundromat, a tiny shop of sausages and meats. I stood in the lamplight, cobbles gleaming. I gazed down the street at the illuminated front of the pink and white church, bathed in its centuries, its quaintness and its historical weight. I wanted dinner and that too played into a shocked sense—a sensibility: here was the present. And here was what history felt like. Here was the rich context of time, the deeds and marvels of my own kind, accumulated into something like a soil, a humus. Where people lived. Where I lived.

It was context in which I was just another human, on his tiny path through time. With all the others.

It was the deep present.

There was a feeling in this moment that I recognized, oddly—something I had felt and treasured from my life in the woods, the obsessive hiking in the High Sierras that had begun exactly in those teen years. What I got up there, what I still get, is a natural context, a sense of the wild unfolding complexity of life. It was a salvation for me in my teens, a way of being, rich and somehow embracing me far more deeply than my puny self-condemnation. In Austria I caught the human version: the wild unfolding context of history, shot through with glory and perfidy. Belonging to all of us.

And I came to see the two contexts as complements. No doubt Los Angeles had left me with voids ready to be filled: LA, where the human story was recent and shallow, where nature had been flattened and, so far as possible, removed. What I felt, in answer to these voids, was the need to live in a rich matrix, a context of depth and breadth, not flatness. So that the smallness of the self might be suspended in a web of meaning: every direction a connection; every connection a mystery, a jewel, a surprise, a world, a wealth. The web of nature. The web of history.

Sehnsucht had led me there. Of course it is often horribly misused. Our political Right imagines a fantasy past and builds of this longing an oppressor's politics of lies and nostalgia. (The old virtues! The old order!) The Left moves its yearning to a utopian future and incites followers with that. (Anyone might be sacrificed on this altar.) Yes, it is easy to manipulate longing.

People are starving to death on this diet of fakery. They ought to be fed the real—though invisible—intangibleness of the deep present, the sublime web of actual connectedness that binds us together now, in this moment. In every moment. The web of natural belonging. And equally the weaving of history and imagination in art, music, and song. These are the inexpressible satisfactions: necessary, fleeting, and impossible to own.

Music eventually taught me that what I longed for was not somewhere far away. Foreignness had nothing to do with it. I did not need to learn German or French, Sanskrit or New Testament Greek. It was no esoteric secret. Every tradition knew about it. All the contemplative Teachers had invited us there, and invite us still.

It is the deep present, as close as breathing, seeing, hearing.

The Pocket Sublime

There's a gallery at the Louvre not mentioned in tourist brochures. It displays no *Mona Lisa*, no giant history painting, no *Winged Victory*, nothing famous. A chamber of nothings, really: just quiet smallness displayed against the darkest of purple velvets in a windowless room.

I found it while walking along the Richelieu wing's second floor, that land of painted wonders, about where it blurs into the Sully wing. I may have been mulling disappointment over the poor Louvre's only Bosch, out for repairs. Or perhaps thinking of a Holbein nearby that reimbursed me in pleasure. Or thinking of nothing at all. I don't recall.

Faces glimmered from a small dark room.

Portrait miniatures: men and women in their Renaissance tunics and dresses, decked out, meeting my glance, content in themselves, *there*. Though hardly bigger than the size of a hand, each little rectangle presented a person's visage, frontal or three-quarters, composed and intense against a plain luminous painted background of light blue or violet-blue or above all a strange glowing green—green of lime, green of tornado weather, green of nothing else I can think of in the world except these paintings. They were framed in tiny wooden fluted columns and wee broken pediments, elaborate, carved, gilded—as if to give them port. But they didn't need it.

What to call these small dignified silences? If it was a sublimity that moved me, it was in a form not described by Burke or Schiller. Something far quieter than waterfalls and thunders, lacking in spectacle and whoop-de-doo. Demure almost. Yet utterly potent.

An hour or two later as I walked the halls toward an exit, I meditated on this impact out of all proportion—this enfolding of scale like a string theory of art in strange dimensions—this closet epic, this pocket sublime.

⟻

William Blake has given us the canonical language for such marvels:

To see a World in a Grain of Sand
And a Heaven in a Wild Flower
Hold Infinity in the palm of your hand
And Eternity in an hour

Everyone has read at least a few of Blake's (deceptively) sweet little verses, especially the *Songs of Innocence*. But Blake's true mania was for epic, his wild attempt to capture the whole enchilada—life, death, humanity, cosmos—in the form of sprawling private mythologies that make the superhero realms of Marvel Comics look dull. They're weird almost beyond description, long and hermetic and obsessive, though occasionally compelling if you give them time. In his epic poems, Blake seems caught up in a whirlwind of imagination from which he hardly knows how to extricate himself. Readers see mostly the mania and back carefully away. So we remember Blake instead for a few perfect little lyrics. In them, Blake has had an outsized influence, memorable, irreducible, and vast.

As a writer of small poems and brief essays, I'm always wondering about the question implied here. Even if a reader does follow me on my brief path of words, does glean some pleasure . . . does it matter? *Can* it matter? A poem is a few puffs of air, seemingly lost in the tornado-winds of commerce and armed wealth, the bloggy smog of vulgarity and noise and blather we live in. Most writers (those who don't achieve best-sellers—that is, nearly all of us) can't help but wonder the implied question of anything fine and quiet: *What's the use?*

There are ways of answering the question. Jesus caught it in the parable of the pinhead-tiny mustard seed, which grows into an ungovernably rangy shrub. I suppose it was a metaphor for faith, but in a larger sense also an affirmation of that realm in which causes and effects are not proportionate. In which, perhaps, the last shall be first, and the meek shall inherit. And small gestures of beauty and integrity might count.

≡

A poet who showed no temptation toward the epic at all was Emily Dickinson. Her entire oeuvre, unpublished save for one verse, was brief haiku-like poems, written in a tiny hand, stitched into pocket-sized notebooks and based on experience enfolded almost entirely within a private garden. Yet her work looms so large it has formed one-half of the foundation of American poetry (sprawling Whitman being the other half). In her work, as in those little paintings, we see what has been called *lyric magnitude*. A paradoxical bigness.

Almost any page of Dickinson's collected poems offers a potential example. Here's one that displays the poet's fey, almost mocking combination of reticence and range:

> To make a prairie it takes a clover and one bee,—
> One clover, and a bee,
> And revery.
> The revery alone will do
> If bees are few.

Within quiet limits, strange depth and expansiveness. As within the confines of a sonnet. Or as in the power of the right word, stroke of paint, musical tone, gesture—to echo beyond all proportion. Duke Ellington, waiting with that one note that seems to pack the whole piece. We could call it the portable sublime. Available vastness: the god of the small and the near.

Perhaps the crucial technology of art is to make this miniature sublime for us. So we need not be limited to that faraway spectacular grove, that remembered night sky, that St. Eustache on the other side of the world. Here, on the bedside reading table or snug in the bookbag, the whole world might be present, its vistas opening dizzyingly before us in the strange inward infinities of the written word.

It was Dickinson, after all, who gave us the key to all sublimities, that inside-the-skull phenomenology that has been my guide and my validation. I don't mind repeating it:

> If I feel physically as if the top of my head were taken off, I know *that* is poetry.

That's the feeling: the sudden scale-pop, the vertiginous intimation of the actual dimensions of the world—or worlds—we live in. When Jean Guillou orchestrates the spaces of architecture and music, that's the feeling. When I enter the redolent spaciousness of an old grove, that's the feeling. Whenever an encounter with nature reveals its wild complexity or its deep-time voyaging or its beyond-imagining power and scale, that's the feeling.

And here is the surprise: even a little flower can do it. Even a little poem. Hubble telescope, meet polemonium. Thunder and lightning, meet haiku. Grain of sand, meet cosmos.

———

Here in Paris, I am reading poetry every day. As I am when at home in Portland. As I was in my mountain-wandering days, when I'd throw a slender volume of Robinson Jeffers into the backpack or sometimes the Kenneth Rexroth translations of Tu Fu and Li Po. Feather-light, dense, intense: these books empowered me to meet the big world all around on equal terms. That was nourishment, that was true feast. That made the heart glad.

Faced with the pomping façades and busy noise of Paris, sometimes I need the same thing. I have a secret store of it, slim and portable, as fit for an overpacked suitcase as for a backpack, and able to walk with me through the gray-skied Tuileries and avenues, awaiting a quiet moment resting in a pew or sipping a coffee.

Often I choose an unsung Northwesterner, Robert Sund. He brings the tall silence with him, shore and cove, stone shingle and cedar grove. He was an unobtrusive guy, writing small lyric poems and playing with brush and ink to capture the essential in the fewest of strokes:

Ink whose body is a river,
whose fullness is
to be joined with other waters

There is a lot of Tu Fu in him, I think. His territory was the Puget Sound country of Duwamish and Snohomish—what he called the "Ish country"— of snow-capped volcanoes and berry-tangled beaches, of rivers, forests, storms, and night skies. And in the midst of it all, Sund, warming himself in a small room with the small lamp of poetry.

The evening light fades through the clouds.
A string of geese calls me out
to sing a farewell, and
I wish them luck as they go from Ish River,
away out over the ocean,
long long sweeps of rippling wings
bound for Siberia.

Their wild song they take with them,
and leave some behind.
They leave enough so
I don't have to leave home any more.

Elsewhere he sketches his actual inkwell in brushy strokes and captions it in
his free calligraphy:

Somewhere in this ink bottle
There is a starry sky.

Aids to reverie. The counterweight to literalness. The evidence of faith. The
pocket sublime.

Cy Twombly: Do Not Say

I love the ugliest painting in the world.

Why? It is inept, unfinished. Five or ten harsh scratches: two eyes, a line of English, a Greek story few of us recall with any certainty. (Who? Which one was he?)

The scrawled eyes are really mere pools of red scribble. There is no face. There is crimson, there is black. Letters badly made.

What is its power, then? From what place is it reaching me?

This painting is not just unfinished. It is practically unstarted. A few rude gestures on whitened canvas—like the anger or the ache *before* thought, before imagining, planning, executing.

(*Do not say executing.*)

—

Cy Twombly is not my usual territory, not my kind of art at all. I do not want to see someone's sketches, notebook, "process." Do not show me your goddamned first draft. *You* do the work: the shaping, deciding, editing. The revising. You, not me.

Spare me the hipster casualness, the tossed-off bullshitty gestures. I have seen them by the acre and never been moved, never, by unordered clutter masquerading as submerged profundity. Pooh. It's easy, it's lazy, and it doesn't speak.

Sophomores shove their midnight poetry at me, shy and hopeful. "And what poetry do you *read?*" I inquire, with seeming innocence. None, of course. They don't want to read poems, or even write them, not really—certainly not rewrite them, nor think about them, nor place them in relation to other poems, much less to other readers who are, you know, actually separate people not locked in the delicious embrace of *their* feelings, that night, that moment. In a month, they will have lost interest themselves, these writers. For now, they cry, "But that's how I *felt*. And that's my *style!*" But no "style" is actually present. Just the innocence of blurt, the automatic writing of the moment, the charmless "self-expression" that is so widely and so mistakenly believed to justify all.

But this. This is what comes before the first draft, call it Draft Zero: the shock, the intake of air and grief, unsought, unhoused, realer than air, realer than flesh and light. Darkness naked as truth.

And the awful news that comes next: that it hasn't killed you, you're still here, while all around you is ashes. Still here, in the space outside of hope, time, proportion. Lost. And yet still here.

ACHILLES MOURNING THE DEATH OF PATROCLUS, reads the scrawl across the painting's lower half.

No one is ennobled here. Death is here. And the grief of a comrade or perhaps lover, red with rage. That is the only color, in two linked red blotches, scribbled. And the charcoal of letters fisted in. The whole of an arm has scored them there. Behind this is a body made tangible. Provoked. Evoked. A body in pain.

(*Do not say body.*)

≡

I saw this painting some years ago, displayed in a group of work that Twombly had spat out in the 1960s. *Vengeance of Achilles. Leda, Swan. Proteus.* "Classical themes" would be the conventional phrase, but these . . . I saw them at the Met. All of them raw, demanding, breaking my resistance. I stared. Was troubled. Walked away, but kept this Achilles, especially, as unfinished business. Did not particularly want to think about it. But could not forget it.

And here it is again at the Pompidou. I am shocked at how untempered it is by time, how hopeless, how immediate. For in the meantime, have I not learned resignation? Learned, even, to be satisfied, to feel the losses of my age and epoch and yet, a little, to take comfort? Not Achilles. Not Twombly. Not on this canvas. Not in another decade, not in a century. Not ever.

I am not reconciled to it. It opens a doorway I have walked through and cannot walk back, though I would if I could. I do not want this.

≡

Because "this" will kill you. Yes it will. Probably we all know this moment: The floor dropping away, the freefall, no hand extended. No exit, no end, no god. Just pain.

I have dragged myself out of it once, twice, yes thrice. I am old, it is all inevitable, uninteresting as mud, good luck and bad luck, hearsed and rehearsed, details this way or that way but all the same, our story, all of us, isolated, all the same and utterly alone. Somehow I came out and lived on. I had strength to burn, and I burned it. Probably that's what this *Achilles* is all about: the uses of strength. (The uselessness of strength.)

I can say I was lucky, was supplied somehow with what was needed. But can anyone say that it was worth it? Can anyone say it was not too hard, ungodly hard, terrifying, destructive, stupid? Can anyone say they will survive another round, meaning, of course, *the next round?* Since it is coming. Oh yes, it certainly is.

Achilles in his strength. A loss greater than any strength. Red blood. Something burned down to soot. All else gone white, vision tunneling as if you would faint. But you don't.

This is the hard bedrock on which Twombly has staked these canvases, pinned them there like victims beneath a pitiless sun. This is grief as spasm, as come-cry, as drowning in a dream and waking to worse. They do not hide, these canvases, do not pretend, do not make peace. They are irreducible.

This toughness is their transcendence: the truth, unsoftened. I have craved truth telling all my life, and here it is. So I am grateful. Yes: grateful. I feel a kind of surge, an animal spirit in this directness: the sublime as beast. Let the blood flow. Let the killing resume; or pause as it sometimes does. We the living—the Not Yet Dead. We will spin and boil, our eyes will look exactly like these eyes scored into the canvas, fierce love and hatred slanting out of them. We will couple in the shadows and even in the broad of day. Let the swords come. Let the pangs and betrayals come. Let the desiring and the losing and all of it come. Childbirth, terror, moneymaking, victory, humiliation, dissolution. We will feel it all, until we don't. And then it is over.

But this canvas is not exactly over. For how many generations will it stare and disquiet? Like sudden torches and shouting in the night, and you ask yourself, *Is this the dancing and reveling?*

Or is this the bloodletting?

The sound comes nearer, nearer. You'll know soon enough.

(Do not say enough.)

Reading in Paris

Overnight rains seem to have ceased just for me to take my mid-morning stroll. A blade-slim volume of Adrienne Rich's poetry rides in my rain jacket pocket, and in low-angle sunshine the streets dazzle. It is the kind of morning that demands something be made of it. If I were a bird, I'd be singing my fool head off. But as usual the puzzle of Parisians tempers me. The well-dressed and the apparently important, rushing in their big-city way. Shoppers, workers, wanderers, even at this hour. And that staggering bum—not my friendly one—always loitering in the cobbled alley rue des Barres, my habitual route, with its oddly hidden big church.

The obscure demand of city life: what, after all, have we to do with one another?

Today at the last minute I have slung on my book bag too. There is a hunger for politics I can't quite account for, and so I bring Václev Havel, *Disturbing the Peace.* And if he comes, then Rich's book of essays clamors to come too, subtitled *Notebooks on Poetry and Politics.*

Poetry and politics. Aren't they supposed to be opposites? The pure and the polluted, the elevated and the debased? Day by day, I read and wonder. We—Rich and Havel and I—cross the rue St. Antoine and head for La Favorite, where I have a chance at that corner table to spread out on. Back sheltered, Paris sidewalk before me, both in the hustle and outside of it, watching with a side-curved glance. Reading, thinking, trying out words.

≡

To be reading in Paris is probably another strange failure to party.

Or else a shocking luxury. I recharge myself daily this way, recalibrating after all that input of museums, crowds, shuffling queues at boulangeries, boulevards of everyone imaginable, languages overheard, semi-grasped. I love all that but . . . here's a poem in my hand. In my mind. It does for me what music does: it stills and cleanses. If I miss a day I feel it. And if two days, then it's like a lack of sleep, the mind's eye gritty, squinting. I may find it hard to be decent to my loved ones.

A private necessity. And yet here I am reading it in the most public of places.

Rich comes to hand, a poem from *The School Among the Ruins*. She wrote it during the George W. Bush war years, that outbreak of American-ism, that time of "tone-deaf cutloose ego swarming the world." In those years, how I struggled in my life and mind! What was the just and necessary response of the citizen of a warlike and undemocratic regime? In her poetry, Rich too struggles.

If all we would speak is ideology
believable . . .
—and I came to think it true indeed I know
I who came only for milk am speaking it : though
I would stand somewhere beyond
this civic nausea

Yes, I recognize that. How in time of war we become lost from one another. Propaganda deafening us like a cloud of white noise. Torture in our name wrenching the spirit. Our leaders twisting logic until it all makes sense. And so we are lost. (And it happens in times *after* war too, I have noticed since. In times of greed. In times of torpor. Or of poverty. Or wealth. That is: *all* times.)

So the poet stands, momentarily bewildered:

but who   at the checkout this one day
do I address   who is addressing me
what's the approach whose the manners
whose dignity whose truth
when the change purse is tipped into the palm
for an exact amount without which

Just like that she ends it, thin-air, not even a period. If I have paid you, why are you still looking at me? Are we not done? What that old Victorian crank Thomas Carlyle called the "cash nexus": human connection thinned and ab-stracted down to this. Coins in the palm. Coins on the eyes. We're done here.

Yet we're not. Something nags, it won't let us be.

Suddenly I remember Barry Lopez's book *Resistance*. I read it back around the war time when Rich wrote hers. The questions are plaintive, and they are my own now, memorized. *Our dilemma is simple: we cannot tell our people a story that sticks. How to write a sentence that might break through?*

How optimistic, to commit poetry in such times. (In all times, in other words.) Even if it is only to ask the question:

> will it matter if our tenderness (our solidarity)
> > abides in residue
> long as there's tenderness and solidarity

Is our tenderness, our solidarity? The words are so sweet I can't yet believe them. But they make me see that my perpetual Paris malaise of unrootedness is really only an exotic version of my usual condition: askance from my fellow humans, observing from the edge and ready to bolt. Paris or Portland, always that disconnect. Or the threat of it. Since coming to Paris I have read far, seeking in an indirect way to place my condition inside something: politics or history or at least understanding. I started with a novel of James Baldwin, that Paris expat, that damaged, fearless truthteller. And Flaubert, his Paris novel set in the exact moment when Marx was seething in his 1850 despair, his Umpteenth Brumaire moment. I read Flaubert to get myself inside the feeling of betrayal and hope mixed with public stupidity. It felt bracing, clarifying to see our same catastrophe, the one we too have known, our shared life, our politics. So I read further, tried to match up these perceptions with those of Václav Havel. And I kept sampling the Left newspapers, frantically denouncing the mini-Brumaire of François Hollande.

Rich's poems brace me, her struggle, thought by thought. So when I feel ready I close the poems and open her book of little essays that are almost like letters. They feel personal, addressed to me. Asking rather than judging. (Maybe prose is inherently more forgiving?) The question for a poet, she says "is how to bear witness to a reality from which the public . . . wants to turn away." Yes, just the point Lopez was making.

Yet, though we may be in public denial, "privately and in secret" we are all feeling the same queasy uncertainty, the near panic. *Can things really be going so wrong?* we ask.

> [T]hese thoughts and feelings, suppressed and stored-up and whispered, have an incendiary component. You cannot tell where

or how they will connect, spreading underground from rootlet to rootlet till every grass blade is afire from the other. . . . Poetry, in its own way, is a carrier of the sparks, because *it too comes out of silence, seeking connection with unseen others.*

I feel oddly validated to learn this disconnect is not mine alone. The way I usually feel is if anything *too* tender—but in a selfish way. As if I did not belong to the madding crowd, was not myself the greedy one. And yet to think of poetry, that most inward of art forms, as a counterforce against such disconnection!

⇒

To my delight, I find Rich commenting on Havel's classic essay "The Power of the Powerless," and there is the Havel, thrown into my book bag beside her! A little synchronicity like this always raises a buzz, an illogical shimmer. As if I were really, in my wandering, on some kind of path.

Rich turns to Havel for the same reason I do: to work out the relation (if any) of poetry and politics—or what she calls "the distance between language and violence." Václav Havel of course was the Czech playwright-poet who led a long-running opposition to the communist state. Imprisoned for it, though never fully muzzled. In the end, he became the democratically elected president. So Havel knows resistance if anyone does. He knows silence, he knows language, and he knows power. Rich quotes him at length:

> The profound crisis of human identity brought on by living within a lie . . . it appears, among other things, as *a deep moral crisis* in society. A person who has been seduced by the consumer value system . . . and who has no roots in the order of being, no sense of responsibility for anything higher than his or her own personal survival, is a *demoralized* person. The system depends on this demoralization, deepens it, it is in fact a projection of it into society.

In my own copy of Havel I have underlined the same passage. Probably everyone who reads it does so. In the same famous essay, Havel makes clear that the seemingly local desperation of Communist Czechoslovakia in 1978 is in fact our universal predicament.

And in the end, is not the grayness and the emptiness of life in
the post-totalitarian system only an inflated caricature of modern
life in general: And do we not in fact stand . . . as a kind of
warning to the West, revealing to it its own latent tendencies?

The essence of this grayness, Havel says in a later book, is the secret
desperation for something real—something not propaganda, not advertising, not sloganeering: "hunger for truth, for a truthful word, for genuine
values." This hunger, Havel teaches me, is fundamental. It is the longing for
living in truth, a longing that usually has no voice, a silence we all learn to
keep.

Poetry, the quietest of arts, answers in that silence. Poetry *that comes
out of silence, seeking connection with unseen others.* Poetry that is the lifeline
to that drowning need for something real, for something truly felt and clearly
seen. Poetry that is, Rich says, the "most portable" challenge to authority, and
the "most concentrated." (Yes: that portable, pocketable sublime!)

To illustrate this concentrated realness and its potential for public
explosion, Rich imports into her essay a tiny eight-line poem from Emily
Dickinson. (She has her Dickinson, I have mine!) It is a fiery secret within
the softly folded precincts of a poem:

On my volcano grows the Grass
A meditative spot—
An acre for a Bird to choose
Would be the General thought—

How red the Fire rocks below—
How insecure the sod
Did I disclose
Would populate with awe my solitude.

By this measure, poetry is a submerged and subversive vastness.

When I was in graduate school a long time ago, freshly and unthinkingly
committed to the life of language and aesthetics—feelings on a page, any
sonnet or sonata that moved me, music always in the back of my mind—my
evangelist brother challenged me. "What is all this for? Is it just some kind of

complicated pleasure?" I had just spent six months learning to read Chaucer in the Middle English of the 1300s. Useless, pointless. My brother was just about to go to Africa to bring material help to villages full of distressed (and unsaved) people.

And I had no answer. What *was* the larger use of this life of reading and scribbling? I was shocked at my inability to know my own apologia. What was I really doing, what did it mean, if anything?

It took me a long time to unravel the question and formulate an answer. And Havel lays it out about as well as anyone. Within the life of conformity to the system, of gray obedience and official mendacity, Havel sees an invisible dimension, a "second culture" which he also calls the "hidden sphere."

Havel writes: "Under the orderly surface of the human life of lies, therefore, there slumbers the hidden sphere of life in its real aims, of its hidden openness to truth." It constitutes a submerged kind of resistance, unspoken yet fully visible, for "opposition is every attempt to live within the truth . . . everything in which the genuine aims of life go beyond the limit placed on them by the aims of the system." (A slumbering force beneath a tranquil surface. Havel could be reading Dickinson!)

The relevance of these words must be clear to anyone living in our current system of runaway global capital, ceaselessly unmaking the world in its blind pursuit of profit, while consumerism pollutes even our most private moments with disconnected amusement, advertising, the ceaseless feeding of meaningless tidbits to the avid, undernourished mind. The hidden sphere/second culture is a "struggle to expand the space" available for that realer life, that felt and truthful response.

And Havel rather tremendously insists: it is not only poets and artists who create the hidden sphere. *Any* work of integrity and attention to detail may silently contribute, for "every good piece of work is an indirect criticism of bad politics."

> teachers . . . clergymen . . . painters, musicians and singers who practise their work regardless of how it is looked upon by official institutions; [and] everyone who shares this independent culture and helps to spread it.

Havel sees a submerged human potency, resilient and always seeking expression. Though anyone's work might contribute implicitly, it is the explicit mission of poetry, and all the arts, to give voice to this silent sphere, this second culture. Not just in overtly "political" works, but in any work that speaks truly of the human condition.

This is the response called for by my brother's not-ill-intentioned question, though I couldn't give it at the time. The life of attentiveness to beauty and truthful expression is in fact a commitment to the hidden sphere. Such a life in fact *practices* the faith that in this invisible way, the human spirit nourishes and advances itself, in contrast to (and inevitably, in opposition to) the surface economy of wealth, consumerism, lying, pretending, shaming, and coercion that seems to govern the world.

This is why, as Rich observes, it is always the imagination "that must be taken hostage" by the official system—"terrorized, sterilized." Poetry and music will always contain the secret answer to power. It is poetry and music that, somehow, even prisoners in terrible straits know are too important to do without. Music arising amid the smoke of extermination camps. Poetry carved into the walls of immigration holding-camps. Songs sung even by the shackled.

And this is Rich's rebuke to the ideological dead-end of Theodore Adorno, who declared that after Auschwitz, poetry was impossible, "barbaric." Rich answers that "surely the Holocaust itself . . . demands a renewed vision of what art—poetry in this instance—stands for and stands against." It is merely another barbarism to rule out poetry, music, beauty: moments that take us to an undefinable other space not for escape but for the practice of being human. No provocation of history can be allowed to erase these, no package of highly wrought intellectualism.

Whatever cleanses the doors of perception, that is poetry. And that is politics. Whatever word awakens the anesthetized soul, quickening the dead shoots with the beautiful cruelty of April, that is the danger that no regime can stand against for long. Even consumerism must yield to it. Eventually the hunger is too strong—the hunger for something true, something real, something felt and inward and shared across the boundary of imprisoning individualism (or collectivism). That is poetry, art, music.

Poetry is the tenderness of solidarity.

=

At La Favorite, I uncross my long legs, raise my eyes from the printed page. People step by on the wet winter sidewalk in ones and twos, scarved and hatted and busy in the business of living. Beneath the visible, there is something else. If you look at the faces, sometimes you might be reminded.

Picasso: Public and Private

The next day, to stretch my legs after a long day of writing and a session at the piano, I walk back across the rue St. Antoine and up the rue Vieille du Temple. I'm thinking of that red-awning'd place full of regular folks and students—what was its name?—with a perfect window-counter seat where I can think and watch people passing and have a late-afternoon beer. On the way I detour over to the Musée Picasso, just to check. Of course closed. It has never been open, not once, in any of my Paris visits or sojourns. It's always tangled in disputes, heirs, money. Funny how quickly cant and self-interest close in over the heads of the poets and imaginers.

Oh yes, here's my café: Le Perle. Of course.

Alongside Rich and Havel, Picasso has dominated my reading this month. *Art* and politics: an especially difficult version of the same question. Today I have carried Russell Martin's splendid book *Picasso's War* about the renowned *Guernica*, which was painted just over the Seine from here in the Latin Quarter in 1937. It embodies exactly what Havel and Rich have declared: how good work, attentiveness, and the life of the imagination offer, in the end, the most potent answer to the lies and repressions of the official system. *Any* official system.

In January of that year Picasso was commissioned by the embattled republican government of Spain to create a piece for the Spanish Pavilion at the Paris International Exposition the following summer. Soon the world was stunned by reports of Generalissimo Francisco Franco's horrific attack on the Basque town of Gernika. From the air, the attack was carried out by warplanes of the Third Reich, which used the occasion to test their new-made weaponry. They bombed and strafed the town into a bloody rubble. And Picasso determined to make it the subject of his painting.

I saw *Guernica* in Madrid at the Reina Sofia long ago, just a few years after its return from exile. Of course, it had become the symbol of Spanish democracy, kept first in France and then in New York and never to be repatriated—at Picasso's insistence—until Franco and his government of brutality had been replaced and repudiated. *Guernica* was in fact my first, puzzled confrontation with the art-and-politics difficulty. The painting wasn't beautiful. It seemed cartoony in its black-white-gray, more graphic than fine-artsy. Yet it struck deeply. I had no idea how to process it.

Most of *Guernica*'s initial viewers had similar problems. The huge painting (more than twenty-five feet wide) hung in a prominent spot in the Spanish Pavilion. It was hard to miss, and it offered a vivid rebuke to the overweening tower and fascist symbols of the neighboring Nazi pavilion. Yet hardly a word of response emerged. The painting went in, the summer visitors drifted by, and . . . "torpid indifference," says Martin. "Hardly anyone was interested. . . . The Spanish Pavilion wasn't even listed in most of the official guidebooks and catalogs of the exposition."

Even the leftist journal *L'Humanité* found nothing to say about it. A few prominent voices did rise, but only to criticize its lack of attractiveness. The famous architect Le Corbusier sniffed (in print) that "*Guernica* saw only the backs of our visitors . . . for they were repelled by it." Not pretty, not attractive, not what one expected. Martin records that some in the (anti-Franco) Spanish Embassy thought it should be "replaced by an artwork that made a stronger statement about the terrible truths of the Spanish war."

The embassy wanted propaganda, the public wanted something comfortable and anodyne. Neither got what it wanted. Yet in time, *Guernica* would be recognized as perhaps the most intimately political expression ever created. It stands with Goya. It has played a role on the world stage few artworks can match, a decades-long international rebuke to fascism and now a symbol of the nation itself in its democratic renascence.

Picasso was a strange choice of prophets. Martin reports that he was apolitical during most of his life, giving at best "lip-service" to politics. He had refused to publicly denounce Franco. He dwelt, it seemed, only in his own visual and imaginative world (though he certainly knew how to make money and fame out of it). The doubters at the embassy "believed he could do little in response to the crisis but issue a private howl."

And indeed, *Guernica* itself, both the finished version and its many preparatory drawings, offers not one image from the actual conflict, not one airplane bomb or soldier, in fact not a single thing from the modern world (except that glaring light bulb near the center of the canvas). It offers instead the imagery Picasso had already been developing, his perhaps obsessive inner mythology: the Bull. The Horse. The Woman. Assembled, of course, in that agonizing scream of pain.

Over the following weeks in Paris, I carry the example of *Guernica* with me. It is there in my mind during a trip to the Pompidou, where modern painters turn the knife of politics and social change, sometimes inscrutable, sometimes charming (in particular that bronze Picasso grouping on the balcony terrace). And during a return to the Louvre, where I visit the gigantic history paintings in the other wing (*Raft of the Medusa!* *Liberty Leading the People!*), then peep in again at those miniature portraits—those exquisite, quiet portraits: men and women whose private magnetism and mystery are brought right into the midst of public view.

And I begin to see. *The artist's canvas is the smallest of public squares.* Six inches by four, or twenty-five feet by eleven, it seeks to exist in the public realm. Even if private and idiosyncratic, it can enter the current and course of shared life: inviting dialogue, comment, reflection, accusation. A painting may be as public as any *place* or plaza.

But this miniature public square is "critical space" only potentially. As with poetry, it depends on how the work is worked, how the moment is seized. I know for sure that no poem that is *merely* private is likely to be cared about by the rest of us. Only when the private urgencies of life are brought into contact with our common life, only when we are invited to share, to be shocked, even to walk away in a huff, only then is the work truly alive. There is always a challenge in it, somewhere. Some glint in the eye, some set in the jaw that invites (or demands) engagement.

The real objection to blandly "normal" art is that it merely supports the norms of the moment, the ways we've made peace with outrage and injustice: that is, the ways we've stopped seeing them. Most of our shared life is bumpered and cloaked with layers of comforting delusion. Predictable art becomes just another deadening layer.

But surely the point of a painting, or a poem, is to jab sharply enough to wake somebody up. And I don't mean just art directly about politics. No, even a sweet little lyric can cut through the husk of habitual inattentiveness. Subject matter is not the question. In fact, producing explicit political stuff is usually a terrible idea, *Guernica* being the great and rare exception. (And even *Guernica*, recall, failed as propaganda: it refused to exclude the "merely" private, just as it refused to repeat the agitprop slogans.) But whatever awakens genuine feeling, whatever stirs us beyond our habitual limits, that is the political. Fiery forgettable candidates and catch phrases may be somewhere far off, yet the work of politics gets done. Quietly. (Or noisily.) But subversively.

And what is the work of politics? Wrestling with that unresolvable point of contact where the private self stands in a crowd, in a community, among other humans, and faces this fact of life: that every human is a half-public beast, a delicate private sensibility roaming in a herd of like animals, sharing their breath and blood and fate. The artist's vision is precisely where this edge can be sharpest: the personal honed to molecular pointedness against the rough realities of our life together.

Of course it hurts. Of course it demands. Of course we cannot live without it.

≕

Picasso's friends rallied to the defense of the painting over the summer. Christian Zervos, longtime editor of the influential art journal *Les Cahiers d'Art*, organized a double issue about *Guernica*. The work began to take its place in the world's imagination.

Three quotes to landmark this unfinishable topic—how the private act of reading a poem or viewing a painting transports one into public space. Three quotes: from Picasso himself and from two of those friends who looked into *Guernica* that summer and found the famously personal imagination of the painter pulled out, everted, into this intensely public moment. Moment that seems to last indefinitely. Moment that still moves and changes viewers generations later.

Picasso:
> Painting is not done to decorate apartments. It is an act of war.

Michel Leiris:
> Picasso also writes our letter of doom: all that we love is going to be lost, and that is why it is necessary that we gather up all that we love, like the emotion of great farewells, in something of unforgettable beauty.

Paul Eluard:
> There is surely another world. But it is in this one.

The Enormous Alphabet [memnoir]

She was always sitting, stooped and motionless, in the cherry rocker with its dark polished wood. I would touch its smooth curves with my fingers and wonder whether she was awake, or (hard to think it, frightening) even alive. I was six. The room as I remember it perfectly still and heavily curtained. Then her eyes would open, watery bright, with a small, reassuring wag of the eyebrows.

When she turned one hundred, President Eisenhower called her on the telephone. I wasn't there but the newspaper had a picture. Seated, stooped, bright eyed.

She had seen the Lincoln funeral train. She saw it herself as it passed through Philadelphia when she was a little girl hardly older than me.

She was dead within the year. She just disappeared. I never saw her buried. Suddenly no Great Grandma. No Nellie. That was how our family handled such things. Her rocker was redone with new fabric and moved to the TV room.

But during the year she lived with us, she became a part of something indelible in my life—an obscure part, difficult to parse. Part of a dream I had at that time that was the most powerful, clear, and insistent of my life.

I don't know if the dream was truly formative, the way people think of dreams as being powerful, as shaping things. Probably it simply announced the obvious. Either way, it remains a sort of permanent vision, a life-dream that mapped my future, that read out to me who I would be and what would dominate, defeat, and nourish my mind for as long as I had one.

≡

It was before Disneyland, before Davy Crockett, before the school assembly about rockets and satellites and beating the Soviets. So the dream had to have come during the era of Sheriff John, a noontime necessity for kids my age in the LA area. He was kindly and reassuring between cartoons and Nestlés commercials (with their disturbing chocolate-colored puppet, doglike, ducklike, that sang out the letters of their brand name with its beaky, furry mouth that rapped shut at the end with a horrible snap).

Or more exactly, it must have been about the time I began *missing* Sheriff John every day. So that was first grade, exciting enough in itself. Engrossing. Astonishing. And I still had Sheriff John on Saturdays.

Our teacher Mrs. Bell seemed somewhere between motherly and grandmotherly to me, plump in that Mamie Eisenhower way in a dark neat dress and black grandma shoes. But she was calm and capable as she guided us, reproved us ("David, stop talking"), or rewarded us with the red curly-tailed monkey stamp, gleaming at the top of the page when you had done well.

I liked to do well.

≡

Nellie's family was Philadelphia Quaker, and it must have been educated and reasonably prosperous. Later on, her sons were given the rather posh names of Bartram and Arlington—*Bartram* to recall their famous ancestors whose botanical garden was still a city treasure, planted by John Bartram with his Royal Patent before the Revolutionary War. *His* son William was apparently difficult to corral, though possessing his father's passion for botany. He was errant in his habits, unmarried, hardly employable. Instead he took long plant-gathering walks in Florida and the Smokey Mountains and the Carolinas, talking to Indians and townsfolk and farmers with democratically equal interest, jotting his notes and sleeping under trees. His book redeemed all, and it is still lively and readable today. People call it Bartram's *Travels*.

About Nellie herself I really don't know much. Evidently a smart-enough girl, she went to normal school—teacher's college—and married a man from Ann Arbor, living there and raising her sons and my mom's mother. At some point Nellie's husband had his bad fall, and so Nellie took charge, no problem. In time her daughter had bad luck too: married a doctor who died young, leaving her alone with the little daughter who would grow up to marry my father. So Nellie moved in to help. Probably took over. Probably a good thing. They made their way to Los Angeles in the 1920s as so many did, hoping to make a new life: one simple-minded husband, one indulged six-year-old, one real widow and one virtual one already getting old yet ever capable, ever willing. That was Nellie.

And then they were both aged and alone together. My grandma and great-grandma lived in two rooms, which my father provided them on a busy street in the inland Los Angeles suburb where we lived—the heavy curtains blocking out noisy traffic and hot afternoon sun that beat against their little place. But I could come up the stairs from next door to see them. And I often did. They had three books that I liked, with words and pictures.

≡

I really wonder where my mind was in school. Have I always been this absent-minded, this prone to drifting off on my own? I liked school. I loved talking and shouting and laughing and reading. I loved writing on the brown cheap paper with the wide-ruled lines and the faint dotted line between them, the capital letters so fancy, and the small letters neat with the tops of their little round heads just touching the middle line. Of course I loved it. Why wouldn't I?

Yet there was some kind of trouble. Though to call it "trouble" is exaggeration. It was the merest scuff of childhood, like crying over a bouncy ball or feeling suddenly embarrassed at your T-shirt. Yet—if you can recall—those emotions seemed very real at the time. Very intense, like primary colors. And for sure there was the off-and-on loneliness. That unattached feeling at recess. Who should I play with? Why were the boys so aggressive and stupid? And what in the world was up with those girls, gossiping and giggling their secrets all the time? I often made attempts to understand what was going on with the adults, too. I would turn their explanations over in my head, trying to make the words go into a pattern I could grasp. Often they just wouldn't go, though I knew the words and could chatter like a goldfinch. There was, for instance, the absolutely frightening Friday air-raid sirens that I had heard since I was four. We lived near a school, and the eerie keening came in over our heads from a few blocks away. On TV, I had seen a war movie with bombs that made a descending cry as they fell from airplanes one by one. Was that what the wailing sound was? But where were the explosions? Adults explained, when I asked, but I could not take it in. Later, of course, we learned to hide from them, those bombs, under our desks. Which was actually fun, crouching there and giggling. Unless you tried to think about it.

My trouble was that midway through the year, for some reason, I was demoted from my reading group—from the Blue Birds down to the Red Birds. We met in three circles of little chairs in three corners of the room, segregated by ability or lack of it. I could see those slowpokes the Yellow Birds—no way I'd fall that far. But why had I fallen at all?

Great-Grandma Nellie had spent some years as a schoolteacher, and she had a solution. I was to read to her every day after school. Simple. Every day. By this time she had been moved into our own house. I suppose that our mom had taken up the duty from her own aging mother, but as a kid I didn't give it any thought. There she was in the back bedroom, in the cherrywood rocker. Smiling, once you got her awake.

To one side of her left eye she had a mole. A big one, you couldn't help looking at it. But she told us—my brothers and the three cousin-boys and me—that it was a push-button and that if we touched it (*very gently*, she said) it would make one eyelid blink. It was very soft, as wide as a fingertip. And it worked, too. It made us less shy with her.

How many months did we read together? I don't recall. But in my mind I can see it perfectly, and I know I am returned, seated with the Blue Birds where I belong.

⚌

Did the dream come then, while I was reading to Great Grandma? Or afterward? I don't know. It's not a thing located in time at all. It has simply been there, all these years.

An enormous alphabet hangs in the sky, towering like a row of gigantic flying saucers in a sci-fi movie. But motionless. They are capital letters, broad and blocky and three-dimensional (sans-serif, I'm just now realizing, gazing at them once again). The ABC end is suspended against a blue sky. It is hundreds or thousands of feet above me, but despite its majesty I feel like I could touch it, the letters feel close, almost intimate. The rest of the alphabet marches off toward the mountains in back of our suburb, getting smaller and smaller above the bright familiar peaks until the end floats off into invisible distance. A long, long ways, unending.

There is color: red A, blue B, yellow C. Light-blue of the silent sky, gray-blue of the hills.

A mute and wordless dream—no words, no action, no emotion except my subdued, unquestioning awe. In scale it equaled anything truly vast I could think of, like the Russians bombing us or Jesus coming back in the clouds—both of which we heard about often in church, since those events were certain to be linked. But there was no white horse, no bomb-scream, no blast, no trumpet, no one being saved or damned. Just this silent, unlimited possibility. It was simply there. And it belonged to me.

I have made a life out of words. Never a hesitation: PhD as fast as I could, assistant prof in English straightaway, and writing, always writing, right to this very day and hour. A long stubborn apprenticeship before my first book, trying things out. And ever the windy business of teaching. I think there's been enough good in that. Here and there. And the undoubted joy of books to read, slim volumes of new poets, triple-decker novels, old classics, tomes philosophic, *jeux-d'esprits*. Labors in French ongoing, and German and Spanish too. Yes, a wordy life.

But I have always leaned another, different life against it: a less-visible life of solitude, of mountains and deserts, long walks, days going by with literally not a word spoken, the yammer of mind spinning down slower and slower until finally it revolves just about like the stars do, steady, untroubled. Good to look at, and with a quiet limitlessness.

—

I like to think of little Nellie in Philadelphia on that April day. The crowds must have been intense—all the accounts say so—as the Lincoln Funeral Train took its slow grieving tour from Washington through Philadelphia and then on to Buffalo and Chicago and finally home to Springfield, Illinois, for the burial.

Somehow we know that her father held her up, way up over the heads of all the jostling people, so she could see Lincoln. That sad day, saddest ever. Her little self, looking and taking it all in, bright eyed. So many Americans saw the train. It must have sealed their pact with what had happened, the war, the bloodshed, the price paid for our sins, our slaveholding moneygrubbing heartless American sins. The Quakers weren't afraid of plain talk; they called a thing by its true name. So Nellie must have understood it, in her way. She must have known that someone had been brave, that someone beloved was dead, and that this was life.

I thought of her again when I was thirteen, home from seventh grade with a cold, and grim-faced newsmen were suddenly breaking in to the daytime television reruns with news about President Kennedy. Nellie's story gave me a small foothold, a way of thinking about terribleness and what kind of world this was. She was already a few years dead. By then we lived in a ranch-style house in a new little tract, where nothing bad, or good for that matter, was ever actually seen to happen.

Truthfully, I don't remember a word she ever said. I just see her, sitting, rocking a little. As silent as that alphabet.

St. Eustache III:
Solidarity and the Sublime

April—

The Paris weather improves. Despite raw rainy outbreaks, the sun shines and the tulips appear. The plaza outside the Pompidou Museum is more populated than just a week ago: bright rain jackets, yellow and red umbrellas (tulip colors!), people milling and photographing and listening to guides. I suppose I have become half resident, feeling a bit above all this gawking and snapshotting.

Yet I'm not. It's just that my snapshots are in words.

I arrive at St. Eustache early for an evening concert, and here at the side door are those ever-present sadsacks, begging with their calculated puppy-dog eyes: *pity me, pity me for the love of God.* I suppose I should. Of course, I don't.

But instead of entering here, I take a pensive detour around to the front entrance of the church. It's a wide portico where St. Eustache welcomes more homeless, the shiftless and the crazy and the addicted and the simply unfortunate. Here on the west porch, under the stumpy tower and the completed tower, a brigade of servers provides what the church website calls *solidarités.* I like the word "solidarity," though I've never been very certain about what it means. In this case it means soup. *Soupe.* Feeding the hungry. So much better than pity. And so much better than politics, too (though of course it *is* politics—politics embodied, wordless). Just soup. Every night of the cold months, at 6:30, St. Eustache feeds about three hundred people. Every night. I have read it on the church website, heard it announced at the ends of services, and now here it is.

At St. Eustache there is really quite a lot of *solidarité*: a talking group for the homeless, as well as a chorus and an improv theater—as if they were real people, with actual talents beyond pitifulness. And I know there is social and medical help dispatched to the needy in their homes. And a group for isolated parishioners, the lonely and abandoned, which admittedly sounds Eleanor-Rigbyish but I bet most of them are about my age, only with worse luck. All this is done by volunteers.

I observe the volunteers setting up their kettles and tables for dinner. A cluster of clients sits to one side, eyeing the preparations. The servers are five. Goodness and generosity glimmer here. And, yes, solidarity. I have earned none of these feelings, yet there is a glow, even for me, simply witnessing it. I feel this: three hundred people with warm full stomachs.

⟺

I know there is no *memnoir* for other people's suffering, no paradoxical sweetness discovered in old pain. Only one's own history is available for this rebaptism, this honeyed transformation. I can't glibly dispense it to others, the depths of their darkness unknown to me and in significant ways unknowable (that blank wall I so often experience, that Bartleby sense of the otherness of fellow humans). I can only say that in my own darkness, stars have shone, kindness beyond measure has been offered. In such acts are intimations of the tremendousness built into the world and built into ourselves too. I wish this discovery for all.

But the sublime is not an answer to empty bellies and shattered lives. And so I have to ask: what is the relation of this occasional feeling to the actuality of our human condition, the common certainties of death and pain and loss? Is it just some coincidence that the place where I have come for sublimity is also the site of such solidarity? Such kindness, should I say— such flesh and feeling, such humanity?

⟺

St. Eustache is the church that prosperous merchants built next to their place of business. A place of wealth, heavy with privilege and its blindness. And from the outside it is indeed a weighty and unlovely presence, close to the hideous marketplace of Les Halles and trading gazes with the palatial Bourse where fortunes were exchanged and schemed and lost. And if you explore around inside St. Eustache, sure enough there with comedic emphasis is the tomb-memorial of one "Claude de Bullion" (!) Minister of Finance to Louis-Thirteen. Yes, elaborate, expensive, marble, in a side chapel close by the Keith Haring altarpiece and the Rubens. Yes, Bullion. Louis also made him Lord Chancellor of the "Order of the Holy Spirit" as if even the divine could be gilded and owned. Though Bullion was a close ally of Cardinal Richelieu, he was said to have been buried at night because so intensely hated.

In the Old Testament, the god of wealth who kills his own children is called Moloch; in the New Testament he is Mammon. Moses encountered him as Golden Calf. But the calf is grown up now, and he works on Wall Street: that famous, furious Bull, standing bronze and big as life at the intersection of Broadway and Morris, reminding us that money tramples everything in its way.

In the Christian temples of Europe you will find him often enough: Moloch/Mammon and the worship of his Golden Calf. How many marble-and-gold cathedrals speak, if you are listening, the ritual language of wealth? The land of Spain offers an especially comprehensive view of it, where churches are encrusted with New World slave-gold and slave-silver. Portugal too. Or a famous church in Prague comes to mind, the St. Nicholas beloved of tourism brochures: its dark marble weighted by gold so thick and so heavy it presses down on the spirit. Without knowing a word of history, a visitor receives this message: *We are vast. We are unstoppable. Give Up.* To underline the point, this Moloch-church places huge marble bishops next to the altar, caped and coped, literally trampling upon some humans whose gasping heads loll back in pain and defeat.

A child could understand this message—and weep.

And yes, plenty of Paris churches strike me the same way: ugly expensive relics. I cannot love St. Sulpice, for one, but there are many others. All over Europe are these kitsch church-palaces of deranged privilege, conveying a message of oppressive weight and power—that same message of tyrants and their monuments throughout the ages: the Dalibor prison towering above Prague, the Soviet-realist Leaders looming above boulevards, Napoleon's massive triumphal arch, the scowling Ozymandias sculptures of the ancients. *Consider my works, and despair.*

St. Eustache ought to be another dead zone. But it is not. Its interior is strangely full of light, unexpectedly beautiful in its proportions. And plain, even austere in its style! I don't know how such things happen. "St. Eustache," in legend, was a Roman general who converted to Christianity. His superiors stripped him of power and looked for a suitable torture. They built a bronze bull—yes, another bull—hollow like an enormous cauldron. And in it they placed him with his wife and children. And lit the fire.

Week by week I come here, to the belly of the beast. And yet I am not burned up; my apostasy and unbelief and long pained history don't seem to deter me. Of course, it is for the music: for the clear, unaffected tenor of the cantor, or whatever one calls the layperson who leads the singing, week by week, in his ordinary street clothes and no-flourishes manner. And I come for the organ, of course. Here in this space, with these strangers, against all odds, I have found a largeness that does not crush but that opens the soul. Saint-Seans played here. Franck played here. I understand why.

Can a wealth-church be redeemed? I almost think so. In a side chapel I find a memorial to Vincent de Paul, who spent a decade of his life in this church in the mid-1600s, before it was finished, feeding and clothing the poorest children from the vast surrounding slums. And, as if de Paul had left some kind of indelible influence here, St. Eustache has continued its remarkable works with the poor, the ill, the outcast. It has stood with AIDS sufferers. It stands with the weak and the hungry. Its deeds answer every stupid doctrine, every loveless Vatican bureaucrat, every money-blind burgher. The deeds are realer than the words. Even the sulking history of huge wealth has not extinguished this other thing, this humanity. I think—privately, since I cannot prove such a thing—that this may be why the music of the place uplifts and attracts. Why the church committed its resources to that organ, that organist, that persistent offering of sound and its unpurchaseable mystery. Why the spaces themselves speak to the dignity and potential of the souls who visit. There is a secret commitment here, deeper than dogma or money or power. It breathes.

Maybe just the practice of coming here has been my transformation. Somehow my long personal aversion to all the apparatus of preaching and saving has fallen away, and I'm able simply to sit here and receive.

I ask myself, what is the difference between a moment of sublimity at St. Eustache and, say, that Billy Graham production of so many decades ago? It is that an evangelizing "crusade" creates a show of simulated vastness designed to herd the mind and feelings toward one and only one response: altar call and redemption, framed in a rigidly set phraseology. Like advertising and political propaganda, crusading evangelism aims to control the mind and narrow the target's thinking toward the one defined objective. Its emotions are weirdly deadening to reason and the other dimensions of our shared humanity. But the arts (and perhaps the less hectoring forms of religion too) are the opposite of propaganda. They aim to open up possibilities, not narrow them; they aim to create conscious space. Within these openings, we are *subjects*, not objects of control.

For in the experience of the sublime, we are always out of our depth and far beyond cocksure formulation. All the deepest experiences of life—love, death, suffering—are irreducible to single meanings. They cannot be boxed in and propagandized. They are paradoxical, boundless, wild—savagely personal and often lonely yet at the same time the very substance of our shared humanity, the common experience of all. Experiences of the sublime, whether natural or human made, launch us into this unboundedness, this spacious mystery within which we are explorers operating by faith, by courage, by hope, and even by love.

＝

Despite ourselves, we find ourselves—here and in other places and moments when we scarcely dare to hope. I think of the outburst of hopefulness that followed those eight Bush years of torture and war and lying, how even from the cesspool of American politics, a system appeared that brought (deeply imperfect) healthcare and thus hope and healing to millions of Americans. Millions! Surely there is a sublime in that?

To imagine it is to see a single American, worrying let's say about a swollen ankle, an untreated condition, a child. To see her suddenly receiving care. To feel the touch of a nurse's hand, the reassurance of a doctor, a medicine, a possible healing. To know the sudden spaciousness of not-fearing, the absence of pain. The sudden space cleared in someone's head, heart, life.

And then to multiply that effect by millions. Surely a sublime there, if one can feel it. And if not, why not? Where is the dead nerve, not to feel *that*?

During my sojourn here in Paris, I've been circling and circling these linked questions. What is this tremendous inward-outwardness that has been my healing these many years? And how has it led me, not away into ever more-isolated raptures, but rather *toward* my fellow humans?

＝

We are swarming individuals, joined so mysteriously and invisibly that we probably doubt it. If we are Americans, individualists, we certainly doubt it; we may even believe with Margaret Thatcher that *there really is no such thing as society*. (I don't. But I act that way, half the time.)

So what are we to do, what will be our polity, our solidarity, if we cannot *feel* our togetherness?

Hayden White, a historian I have admired for decades, points out that any large political vision necessarily partakes of the sublime. And that poses a problem for us lefties and liberals, in our search for a way to actualize that earnestly desired solidarity. For of course it is the forces of conservatism that have typically revved up the "sublimity" in their appeals. They have used the phony sublime to great advantage, motivating the public often, it seems, even against its own self-interest. Their large abstractions awaken fervent followings—Liberty, Nation, Flag, God—creating a paradoxical meta-unity of self-declared "individualists" in faceless mobs of tribal conformity. Meanwhile, White says, the great line of leftist thought from Kant to Hegel to Marx took a different road. If the sublime was an agent of right-wing mystification, throwing bogus divinities and divinized traditions in the way of progress, then the left would advocate for something rational, measurable, and scientific: something explicitly non-sublime.

White says that this "demotion of the sublime" required the left to advocate for a mostly rationalist idea of history and change—a technocratic government of betterment. Marx taught the left to expect a steadily improving social condition. The beauty of the leftist program lies in its practical, material justice. No blood-and-soil, no flag, no god.

Yet without a stirring vision, who is really motivated? Where is the feeling of uplift and excitement that can buoy us above and through the slogging, menial labors of actual politics? The logrolling and compromising, the alliances and dealmaking, the weary work of balancing complaints and demands? That is to say, the actual practice of community.

It seems to me that without a strong vision, a *felt* connection to some larger worthiness, this work is simply too dispiriting. The public comes to cynically distrust it, and the best learn to shun it. Politics reverts to self-interested manipulators.

The express belief of the left is *solidarity*: that our human well-being is a shared project. But Reaganite antigovernment individualism has swept away the old liberal consensus, the New Deal and its successors, and is at work right now attempting to demolish all its achievements: collapse the new health-care system, hobble environmental protections, and cut earned entitlements like Social Security as well as measures to help the poor—even as the wealthy become ever more shockingly wealthy and the middle classes stagnate and shrink. The right denigrates the public sphere in all its forms and activities and works ceaselessly to replace it with so-called "individual liberty," which inevitably means letting corporations and their owners take over the actual governance of the world.

Where is the liberal pushback to this orchestrated danger? The left mumbles. It lacks confidence. It seems to have no vision. It compromises before negotiations even start, then capitulates. In France, the Socialist President Hollande is hardly in office before he is pathetically backpedaling and adopting dilute versions of his predecessor's austerity. The limp spectacle is mocked as the "Soft Left" versus the "Hard Right" ("la Gauche Molle et le Droite Dure"). Even France! Which, to many of us in the Anglo-American world, has seemed a touchstone of hope that some other motive besides private wealth might organize and inspire a people. How bitter it is to see the Great Alternative foundering. What shall we do without it?

But then what is the language of our common humanity? Where is the imagery that captures the miracle of beauty, complexity, and generosity that is—truly *is*—our shared social and biological life? The life we have in common is a marvel. Yet our eyes are on our dinner plates, our little stacks of money. We shrink ourselves into the smallest version of humanity, grumbling and canoodling and scheming for private advantage behind closed doors.

=

The practice of politics needs to be organized under a starry sky of aspiration, a connectedness experienced in the heart and bone as a reality not merely a theory, binding citizens mutually in some great hope which they are building—not another descent into the phony sublime. Because the real thing is available.

Working in my last days in Paris (and after Paris too) to complete this manuscript, I find research that recapitulates exactly my own experience with the sublime. Paul Piff, a psychologist and sociologist, and Dachner Keltner, a psychologist, undertook to test the effects of awe. It's remarkable, really: they experimented at a favorite place back in my native California—just where I'm known to bring friends when I visit, trying to share the intense power I sense there:

> Some of this research was conducted on the campus of the
> University of California, Berkeley, which has a spectacular grove
> of Tasmanian blue gum eucalyptus trees, some with heights
> exceeding 200 feet—a potent source of everyday awe for anyone
> who walks by.

Of course, a grove of big trees! That feeling I've been harboring and seeking out and trying to understand for so many years, the better part of my life, actually. And here they are, this stand of immigrant trees, providing an instant, head-tilting expansion into awe, right in the midst of bustling town and bristling intellect and undergraduate nonsense and all.

> [W]e took participants there and had them either look up into the trees or look at the facade of a nearby science building, for one minute. Then, a minor "accident" occurred (actually a planned part of the experiment): A person stumbled and dropped a handful of pens. Participants who had spent the minute looking up at the tall trees—not long, but long enough, we found, to be filled with awe— picked up more pens to help the other person.

> In still other studies, we have sought to understand why awe arouses altruism of different kinds. One answer is that awe imbues people with a different sense of themselves, one that is smaller, more humble and part of something larger. Our research finds that even brief experiences of awe, such as being amid beautiful tall trees, lead people to feel less narcissistic and entitled and more attuned to the common humanity people share with one another.

Interestingly, just a few years before these studies, Piff and Keltner had also done research into an opposite effect: the tendency of wealth to *reduce* compassion. They compared the behavior of luxury-car drivers to that of ordinary-car drivers in yielding (or not yielding) to pedestrians and the like. And they set up other experimental situations that gave the same results. Their conclusion: *more* money seems to produce *less* ordinary compassion and cooperativeness. The shallow allure of wealth somehow manages to subdue the sublime.

So this more recent research into awe suggests a kind of wealth that money can't buy, an available though under-noticed way of being, a more expansive mentality that leads in the opposite direction from the entitled, kvetching individualism of our money-oriented consumer culture.

[W]e suggest that people insist on experiencing more everyday
awe, to actively seek out what gives them goose bumps, be it in
looking at trees, night skies, patterns of wind on water or the
quotidian nobility of others—the teenage punk who gives up his
seat on public transportation, the young child who explores the
world in a state of wonder, the person who presses on against all
odds. . . . All of us will be better off for it.

You can't do better than a phrase like "quotidian nobility"! Here is a kind of
good news so familiar that it stays hidden in plain sight most of the time.
The sublime is not merely a commodity of faraway memories, expensive
vacations, or rarified aesthetics. It belongs equally to daily life. It enriches us
with a sensibility both wider and deeper than the pursuit of wealth can comprehend. It leads us toward each other. When we realize—experience—this
spacious and incomprehensibly mysterious planet, including the mysteries
and graces of each other, we become more than just money accumulators
and consumers. We become humans.

We have seen that the sublime creates a paradoxical inside-out economy
of experience in which an encountered vastness opens an analogous space
within, dizzying in both directions. Perhaps love is the inner horizon of
the sublime, as vastness is the outer. The ennobling experience of solidarity,
the surprise and necessity of love—these occupy spaces of real magnitude
within us.

So it should not surprise us to find, in the practices of faith and the
researches of sociologists, that these two magnitudes, the inwardness of love
and the outwardness of the sublime, are related. They connect in some nonlinear way, the one speaking to the other, echoing and reinforcing. In them
we are driven not to settle for trivialities; in them we seem drawn toward
vistas worthy of our immense capacity for delight, silence, awe, and self-
transcendence. In them we know our smallness, yes, and truly. Yet in them
we brave all, rising toward a greater world, a connectedness with others, a
greater self, an abundance.

I spent Easter Sunday at St. Eustache, in the company of a few hundred fellow travelers. A world of sound opened the space above and around
us. The service rolled forth in French I could understand enough of the time,
even Bible verses I had memorized fifty or sixty years ago in Baptist Sunday

schools turning pleasantly strange in this musical tongue. I believed none of it. But I felt all of it. Not as doctrine. But as mutuality, an experience of the flesh that was not *entirely* self-enclosed. In a crowd of strangers I felt like one of them.

Into the generous light-crossed space around us, the cantor sang out. I did too (a little). The choir gave voice. The organ played. Palestrina, Vivaldi, Telemann. A Bach fugue. Everything, everything, everything.

Epilogue: Getting Out of the Way

It is near the end of our winter and spring in Paris. On the day I turn sixty-four, I am in a house on the coast of Brittany. It has a piano (of sorts) and in a quiet moment—hosts and guests gone for walks—I approach the Schubert Sonata in a mood of tranquility. I have carried my music with me. This is many weeks after the Nineteen Labors began, those (for me) heroically difficult measures on which I have been working, working, working.

And something good is happening. The pathway clears. Diminished-chord instabilities lead to melodies that ring, stay a moment, wander off. And I find I can walk with them, one and all, from beginning to end. Muscle memory guides the fingers and for once I allow it. I let it happen. Yes, I am focused, I must attend; yet it is a floating kind of attention. There is something of a workman's attitude, getting the job done but not thinking too much. More like fishing, perhaps. Not causing a ruckus by your presence, but in a sense erasing yourself . . . while responding to whatever arises.

This getting out of your own way: perhaps it is the core difficulty for a certain kind of person. *My* kind of person.

The mind is a famously busy little monkey, isn't it? Rarely do I find myself unreflectively present. In conversation I may be racing forward, anticipating the rest of the other speaker's sentence, taking the half-second thus freed to consider my response or to analyze whether this is interesting, why or why not, and then to chasten and remind myself to care, or appear to care, and to manifest caring like this (nod) or this (make a concurring noise).

Oh yes, a busy mind.

In performance situations, this kind of busyness can be fatal. How often I make the mistake of *noticing* my own playing—of thinking, *Hey, that went great!*—which immediately leads to, *But what about the next measure?* And then the process is derailed, the mind getting in the way. It is the opposite of grace, this self-mirroring blather. And a guarantee of broken performance.

It is as if *the playing* needs to be its own consciousness. The moments I have spent in this *playing* mind—amazing, that calm sufficiency—that fleeting grace I can so seldom rest in.

To be present in my life. To cease being my own watcher and become instead my deeds. How many years have I paid in self-wounding loneliness, in work that was correct but not inspired, in play that was more task-like than joyous: to ski this well, to walk this far, to climb this high? All under the watchful eye that William Blake called NoboDaddy, and that I sometimes have called Goddy Boy: the accusing eye that sees only the meagerness of one's efforts. (In the end, of course, it proved to be *my own* baleful eye, doing the god/devil's work for free.)

It is a subtle and ironic egotism, this self-defeating self-regarding. Like all egotisms, it is a charnel house where the spirit dies. And only at this end of my life, as the real end approaches, do I begin to find the way out of it.

Ah, but not too late. Not quite.

⸺

Yet I could say that a way out of this dead end has been with me my whole life.

So many moments of joyous abandon and wild abundance! Listening to music, of course. Or, equally well, looking at paintings or sculpture or theater. Reading poetry, novels, nonfiction. And above all, walking into the great otherworld of nature.

All opportunities of awe. The mind expanded, the body liminally warmed, charmed, elevated with a sense of well-being, unearned and unexpected. The *sublime*, we are calling it. Something speaking to me, something inviting me into a larger existence.

Would I have survived without it? Since my childhood, these moments have nourished me and drawn me on. They have forgiven me, wordlessly and untheologically (thus a gift I could accept). I believe such moments build themselves into a person's inner mind, that secret other who shadows us, that better, calmer, older self.

This self can be strengthened, can be attended and patiently awaited. But not summoned. Our relation to it—to Him or Her—is like that of a watcher on the edge of a grove, who hopes to see what emerges, quietly, into the clearing. In my experience—my very long experience as a walker and waiter and watcher, by streams and by glades, on high ground and low— these vigils are never disappointing. Never. Though what appears, that is usually a surprise. Best to come with no expectations, as void and blank-minded as possible. I have seen ants that shook the earth, and me on it. But to see them I had to become light, small, and vanishing myself.

For there is a self-emptying on the approach to the sublime. In the old-fashioned formulation, the sublime experience was, of course, an encounter with vastness of an overpowering, dangerous, and terrifying sort. A rocky chasm, a thunderstorm, a roaring ocean: these, in their awful beauty, spoke to our mortal smallness like Yahweh mocking Job, asking *Where were YOU when I laid the foundations of the World!?* The result was a terrible pleasure, a joy on the brink of dread. The self reduced to nothing, emptied of ego, then filled with a largeness which the mind itself thrills to even half contain.

I seek to expand the term. I have known the sublime, or something like it, in so many other ways than wave-crashing spectacle. But the formulation remains: First the emptying. Then the abundance ... wild, joyous, unsettling, momentary. Unforgettable. Starry-sky abundance.

And we may discover that the abundance comes indoors, comes to live with us, held ever after in some invisible reserve.

═

The Brittany house perches on a hilltop a few steps from a rocky cliff, from which I look down at the *falaise* of coastal path, cliff-side cemetery, brief sand beach between two points. Pines cling to the heights, and below them the ocean foams on boulders and crosses the curving patch of sand, then withdraws to leave a tawny crescent, warm against the cool sea-blue.

Close to the house stands a stone chapel built five hundred years ago to bless fishermen and comfort wives and widows. It is tiny, hardly a one-car garage. Yet having faced the centuries it takes on an undeniable dignity. Its little granite steeple and single doorway bear carved faces and figures smoothed down by wind. A dogface corbel. A coy saint. Rounded off and blurred, they persist, while the green surf sends up a smacking wind as fresh as the first day of time.

Snug inside the house, I approach the little upright piano in a roomy old stone-floored parlor cut open by a modern stairway going up to bed-rooms. Later, at a long table on the other side of the room, we will feast on *plateau de fruits de mer*, mussels and langostino and oysters and whitefish laid out on silver columns and oval trays and platters with legs, the whole thing a shining, lemony-briny marvel. We had it here several years ago and tonight the reprise. I have put two bottles of Muscatel into the *frigo*.

But for now the house is quiet. Sunshine throws bars of light across the room. The hosts are out shopping for our repast, the other guests exploring the *falaise*. I sit to try the little white-painted upright. The floor is so uneven that the piano rocks. I try bracing it with my knees. But to do that, I must balance my heels on a chunk of wood brought up from the cellar, keeping myself steady on the bench while my right foot, heeled firmly, tries to pedal without moving the whole thing too much. The piano holds steady, the wind blows by. I make do in the shaded brightness, the gusty quiet.

The old house shows a definite panache, made new with glass and steel, new art, new rooms. Yet understated, like its owners. Gwen's family has held this house for generations. It gives me pleasure to think of her, a decade at least younger than me and still attractive in that French way, even magnetic: blonde, a tip-touch of blue mascara, a scarf, a subtle tan. She loves the sun of this tiny, fancy town, filled with yachts and cafés. She is elegant and natural in her style.

My partner and I got to know her as director of the small fine-arts college where we had been invited, a few years ago, to teach for a semester (its clientele mostly American, the language of instruction English). How quickly Gwen made us feel comfortable in our new setting! My task was to offer some readings in Rimbaud and Whitman and pose writing exercises that might contribute to the students' (visual) creative process. As the non-artist on the faculty, I was peripheral. My usual posture, I would have rested in it, content. But Gwen insisted on including me, anchoring me in the daily weft of meetings and concerns, drawing me in with a word, a question, a request. (It was a tiny school, so this felt more like community than committee duty.) In fact she kept her eye on all the visiting profs, never forgetting our dislocation, however exciting, in this land of incomprehensible conversation and Gallic aloofness.

I have thought of it often, how Gwen brought this humanity to her professionalism. It is a combination rare in academia, or anywhere, in my experience. I wonder if it is also simply French—the land of long lunches and solidarity. The warmth beneath the reserve.

And our other host, Gwen's Hervé: long and lean, crew cut, smart in a technical way (he works with computers), literate and always reading. He smiled and joked me into a comfortable friendship when my French was even worse than his English. We have both improved now, but still my best French conversations come with him, when we are each swimming bravely in the other's language. I find myself becoming confident, chattering away because, hey, *he's* in the same predicament, searching for a word in English, laughing, finding. These sessions leave me feeling calmly capable, for once, in my earnest French, undefeated.

And now, unexpectedly, I am playing with ease on the rocking piano. (When have I ever done that before, with people listening?) Gwen has returned; she comes in to set down a drink for me in perfect style—a Prosecco for mid-afternoon. Hervé and the other friends are still out strolling. The house falls quiet when I stop playing. Then I start into the big Schubert opening chords, and in unison Gwen and I realize the stemware will never survive an assault of German Romanticism, the little upright teetering wildly. She retrieves the glass in time, deposits it within reach on the flagstone floor, regards me a moment—playing to the silent house, peering intently into my marked and sticky-noted music—and thinks, perhaps, of our last conversation, when I tried to explain to her why I took so many walks by myself, so many high-altitude hikes and adventures. Her English is the best. She lived a year in Seattle after college, working as a barista, fearless of the daily barrage of sloppy American idiom. She seems unsinkable, Gwen. But she looks me over, my long legs tucked at odd angles under her piano. "You're *funny*, aren't you? Funny." I think she's finally found a way to categorize my bookish cool, my awkward savoir-faire.

The piano rocks, the winds blow and pause, the friends and loved ones return. They drift into the late glow of the parlor room, sipping, conversing. And I begin to play for them, too. Unconcerned for my errors, drifting again through my grand challenge the sonata, then moving on to Joplin, not too fast, and Mozart who best fits the instrument's small clear sound. Some of this, some of that. Conversation goes on, and I take care to play under its lulls and laughters. All the while keeping my knees just so, my mind light but focused. And the music—imperfect, human, wandering, discovering—rises and rolls and harms no one, and perhaps in its small way, blesses.

And so to my list of awe, let me add this minor beauty: the company of friends. Unobtrusive but never without its own strangeness. A certain kind of music.

Notes

EPIGRAPH PAGE

ix *l'epouvante fréquent*: Franck André Jamme, *Au Secret* (Plounéour-Menez [France]: Éditions Isabelle Sauvage, 2010), 6.

ix *terror visits*: Frank André Jamme. *To the Secret*, trans. Norma Cole (New York: La Presse, 2015).

ix *We had the experience*: T. S. Eliot. "The Dry Salvages" in *The Four Quartets* (Boston, New York: Houghton Mifflin, 1971), 39. [Originally 1943.]

BALTHASAR DENNER, BILL VIOLA

29 *Woman With a Blue Hood: Balthasar Denner*. Oil on copper (1721–28). Paris, Louvre.

32 *The Quintet of the Astonished*: Bill Viola, *The Quintet of the Astonished*. 2000, Color video rear projection, 15:20 minutes. Paris, Grand Palais.

34 *The historian records: "His convalescence was very slow . . ."*: William Schroeder, "Balthasar Denner (1685–1749): Portrait Artist," *Mennonite Historian* 30, no.1 (2004): 1–2.

MOUNT ST. SUBLIME

44 *National Vow*: Basilique du Sacré Coeur de Montmartre, "The Origin of the Construction of the Basilica, a 'National Vow,'" http://www.sacre-coeur-montmartre.com/english/history-and-visit/article/the-origin-of-the-construction-of.

45 *I stood on a horseshoe-shaped rim*: the blasted-out caldera is a mile across (1.5 km) (http://www.newworldencyclopedia.org/entry/Mount_Saint_Helens), and about 2.5 miles north to south (http://archive.boston.com/bigpicture/2010/05/mount_st_helens_30_years_ago.html.)

46 *Friedrich Schiller*: Friedrich von Schiller, *Naive and Sentimental Poetry and On the Sublime*, trans. and intro. Julius A. Elias (New York: Frederick Ungar, 1966).

46 *James Thomson, The Seasons*: qtd. in Marjorie Hope Nicolson, *Mountain Gloom and Mountain Glory: The Development of the Aesthetics of the Infinite* (New York: Norton, 1959), 358–59.

46 *"writing in the 1790s"*: Elias, "Introduction," 78.

46 *"mixed feeling"*: Schiller, 198.

46 *"a composition of melancholy . . ."*: Schiller, 198.

46 *"the sensuously infinite"*: Schiller, 204.

46 *"fearlessly and with a terrible delight"*: Schiller, 203.

47   *Edmund Burke*: Edmund Burke, *A Philosophical Enquiry into the Origin of our
      Ideas of the Sublime and Beautiful*, ed. and intro. James T. Boulton (Notre Dame,
      IN: University of Notre Dame Press, 1968).

47   *"[T]he sublime . . . always dwells . . ."*: Burke, 113.

47   *"not pleasure, but a sort of delightful horror . . ."*: Burke, 136.

47   *"new printings continuously for the next thirty years"*: Burke (Boulton's intro-
      duction), xxii.

47   *the sublime pushes moral questions into the background*: Boulton makes the point
      that the sublime reinterprets extreme experiences formerly the province of
      tragedy. Tragedy's exploration of *moral* and *ethical* dilemmas, rooted in character,
      becomes the sublime's confrontation with *sheer being*, stripped of moral dimen-
      sion. Burke (Boulton's introduction), lix–lx.

48   *"the spiritless regularity . . ."*: Schiller, 204.

48   *"bizarre savagery"* and *"wild incoherence"*: Schiller, 206.

48   *"Let us stand face to face . . ."*: Schiller 209–10 [emphasis in original].

48   *"the incomprehensible sublime"*: See for example Jean-François Lyotard: "The
      Sublime and the Avant-garde" in *The Sublime*, ed. Simon Morley (London and
      Cambridge, MA: Whitechapel Gallery/MIT Press, 2010), 30.

49   *Gaston Bachelard*: Gaston Bachelard, *The Poetics of Space*, trans. Maria Jolas
      (Boston: Beacon Press, 1969), 184.

BOSCH IN THE BURNING WORLD

50   *dommel*: "Word Reference" (Dutch): the related verb dommelen means "to
      drowse." https://www.wordreference.com/ennl/drowse

50   *St. Anthony*: Hieronymous Bosch, *The Temptation of St Anthony*. Triptych, oil on
      wood panels, c. 1501. Lisbon, Museu Nacional de Arte Antiga.

51   *many scholars . . . elaborate keys*: too many for me to pretend I've done more than
      sample them, including Nicholas Baum, Laurinda Dixon, Larry A. Silver, Walter
      S. Gibson, and Lynda Harris.

53   *Jacobus de Voragine*: Jacobus de Voragine, *The Golden Legend*, trans. William
      Granger Ryan (Princeton, NJ: Princeton University Press, 1993), Vol. I, 93–96.

53   *"Now that I have seen you"*: de Voragine, 93

53   *"How can anyone escape?"*: de Voragine, 94.

54   *An archer once saw Anthony taking his ease . . .*: Jacobus de Voragine, *The Golden
      Legend*, trans. William Granger Ryan (Princeton, NJ: Princeton University Press,
      1993), Vol. I, 94.

54   *two lay brotherhoods*: reported by numerous scholars, sometimes naming
      them with slight differences, including the "Common Life Fraternity" and the
      "Brotherhood of the Virgin" (Baum) and the "Modern Life Movement" (Dixon).

SCHUBERT II: COUNTING TIME

67   *strange attractor*: biographical material is mostly from Christopher H. Gibbs,
      The Life of Schubert (Cambridge: Cambridge University Press, 2000), with
      other details from Lawrence Kramer, *Franz Schubert: Sexuality, Subjectivity,
      Song*, (Cambridge: Cambridge University Press, 1998), and scholarly articles by
      Maynard Solomon.

67   *"sausage-eating"*: Schubert qtd. in Gibbs, 116.

68 *a report that little Franz befriended a joiner's apprentice*: attributed to Schubert's early biographer Heinrich Kreissle von Hellborn. I accessed this detail in Wikipedia: "Franz Schubert." https://en.wikipedia.org/wiki/Schubert. Original source Heinrich Kreissle von Hellborn, *Franz Schubert, a musical biography*, trans. Edward Wilberforce (abridged, 1866) (roughly, volume 1 of Kreissle), 3.

69 *"the requisite interest . . . aversion to music teaching"*: Gibbs, 46.

69 *Otto Erich Deutsch*: Otto Erich Deutsch and Eric Blom, eds., *Schubert: A Documentary Biography*, rev. and augm. and with a commentary by the eds. (London: J. M. Dent, 1947).

69 *"dearest and best . . . everything" to him*: Gibbs, 46.

69 *"Hats, boots, neckerchiefs . . . between want and plenty"*: Gibbs, 124 [brackets and ellipses in Gibbs].

70 *a troubling concern: for instance a typical comment on his "thoroughgoing tipsiness"*: Gibbs, 97.

70 *carry him from the room*: Gibbs, 97.

70 *"genuine dread . . . of philistines"*: Bauerenfeld qtd. in Gibbs, 48.

70 *"ordinary students and officials"*: Schubert qtd. in Gibbs, 120.

70 *"not to be constrained by the conventions of society"*: Joseph von Spaun qtd. in Gibbs, 96.

70 *"I sit here alone"*: Schubert qtd. in Solomon, "Peacocks," 195.

70 *"the countess was somewhat retarded . . ."*: Solomon, "Peacocks," 195.

70 *"my beloved" . . . "I share his whole life with him"*: Schwind qtd. in Gibbs, 118–19.

70 *"dominating aversion to the daughters of Eve"*: Hüttenbrenner qtd. in Gibbs, 37, and see Solomon, "Peacocks," 196.

71 *"always rather reserved in this regard"*: Stadler qtd. in Solomon, "Peacocks," 196.

71 *"Many others report the same thing"*: Among surviving letters from Schubert and his circle, an elevated and passionate language prevails among and between the (male) friends—but not a written word of such intimacy to, or with, any women (Solomon, "Peacocks," 196). Schubert's first biographer, Heinrich Kreissle von Hellborn, concluded rather delicately that regarding the pursuit of women, "with him this tendency was not nearly so much in evidence as it usually is in men of lively imagination" (qtd. in Solomon, "Peacocks," 195). Schubert himself, in a perhaps desperate bid to close off the topic, declared to his parents that he had renounced marriage (Gibbs, 134).

71 *"excessively indulgent sensual living"*: Schober qtd. in Gibbs, 94.

71 *"double nature . . ."*: Bauerenfeld qtd. in Solomon, "Peacocks," 193.

71 *open secret*: see the work of Eve Kosofsky Sedgwick for this foundational concept in queer studies, for instance in *Between Men: English Literature and Male Homosocial Desire* (New York: Columbia University Press, 1985).

71 *"maidenly character . . ."*: Schumann qtd. in Kramer, 80–81.

71 *"Schubert's compositions . . . coquetry . . . effeminate weakness . . ."*: qtd. in Solomon, "Nostalgia," 14, and in Kramer, 81.

73 *"The [music's] space . . . the interior of the head"*: Barthes qtd. in Kramer, 103 [emphasis and ellipsis added].

73 *"imaginary escape from the self-alienation . . . of 'normal' men"*: Kramer, 78.

BEYOND GODDARD CANYON

75   *that Van Gogh:* Vincent Van Gogh, "Fritillaries in a Copper Vase." April–May 1887, oil on canvas, Paris, Musee D'Orsay.

77   *this is Spartacus:* Louis Ernest Barrias, "Le Serment de Spartacus" (The Oath of Spartacus), 1869–1871. Paris, Jardin des Tuileries.

79   *cutthroat trout . . . a million years:* "The cutthroat trout species has ancient roots and began divergences leading to the present diversity of subspecies perhaps 1 million years ago." Robert J. Behnke, *Trout and Salmon of North America* (New York: Chanticleer, 2002), 145.

80   *Edmund Burke:* Edmund Burke, *A Philosophical Enquiry into the Origin of our Ideas of the Sublime and the Beautiful,* ed. and intro. James T. Boulton (Notre Dame, IN: University of Notre Dame Press, 1968).

81   *"beauty . . . some strangeness in the proportion":* Francis Bacon, "Of Beauty," in *The Essays,* ed. John Pitcher (New York: Penguin, 1985), 188.

81   *"Beauty itself is but the sensible image of the infinite":* widely attributed to Bacon, though I cannot locate the original source (if it exists).

81   *"Death is the mother of beauty":* Wallace Stevens, "Sunday Morning," in *The Palm at the End of the World: Selected Poems and a Play,* ed. Holly Stevens (New York: Vintage, 1972), 5–8. [Originally 1915.]

ST. EUSTACHE II: THE SOUND WORLD

85   *speculation . . . 3.5 seconds:* I read this notion three decades ago, an intriguing but utterly nontechnical guess in a book about epic poetry. So it's lost in the mists of time for me (but still an interesting speculation). See William James's estimate below.

85   *William James . . . "specious present":* "the prototype of all conceived times is the specious present, the short duration of which we are immediately and incessantly sensible. . . . We are constantly aware of a certain duration—the specious present—varying from a few seconds to probably not more than a minute." William James, *The Principles of Psychology* (New York: Henry Holt, 1890), qtd. in Robin Le Poidevin, "The Experience and Perception of Time," *The Stanford Encyclopedia of Philosophy* (Summer 2015 Edition), Edward N. Zalta (ed.), http://plato. stanford.edu/archives/sum2015/entries/time-experience/. This is a good general resource on the question of experienced time.

86   *"where the eye divides, the ear connects":* John Luther Adams, *Winter Music: Composing the North* (Middletown, CN: Wesleyan University Press, 2004), 164.

87   *"quality of attention":* Paul Shepard, *Nature and Madness* (San Francisco: Sierra Club, 1982), 21.

87   *"Merely to look. . . . The hunter is the alert man":* José Ortega y Gassett, *Meditations on Hunting,* trans. Howard B. Wescott (New York: Scribners, 1985), 130. [Originally 1942.]

89   *Emily Dickinson . . . top of your head come off:* "If I read a book and it makes my whole body so cold no fire can ever warm me, I know that is poetry. If I feel physically as if the top of my head were taken off, I know that is poetry." From letter 342a to Thomas Wentworth Higginson, collected in *The Letters of Emily Dickinson,* eds. Thomas Johnson and Theodora V. Ward (Cambridge, MA: Belknap/Harvard University Press, 1958). It is also quoted in the introduction to

the widely used collection *Final Harvest: Emily Dickinson's Poems*, ed. and intro. Thomas H. Johnson (Boston: Little, Brown, 1961), x.

90   *We lived like this … twelve to twenty-five people*: The typical hunter-gatherer living unit, according to Paul Shepard's review of the paleoanthropological record. *The Tender Carnivore and the Sacred Game* (New York: Scribner, 1973), 103–07. Much of Shepard's work was concerned with the present implications of our deep physical and social evolutionary past. A fine compact summary of his work is the posthumous *Coming Home to the Pleistocene*, ed. Florence Shepard (Washington, DC: Shearwater/Island Press, 1998).

90   *several hundred thousand years*: the horizon of human fire use has been pushed back well past the appearance of *Homo sapiens*. Ron Shimelmitza, et. al.,"'Fire at will': The emergence of habitual fire use 350,000 years ago," *Journal of Human Evolution* 77 (2014): 196–203.

SCHUBERT III: CHANGING MY MIND

94   *neuroscientist Gottfried Schlaug and his associates*: Oliver Sacks, *Musicophilia: Tales of Music and the Brain* (New York: Knopf, 2008), 94.

94   *Alvaro Pascual-Leone*: Sacks, 94.

95   *Lisa Feldman Barrett*: "What Emotions Are (and Aren't)" *New York Times*, 2 Aug 2015, Sunday Review: 10; and see Barrett's *How Emotions Are Made: The Secret Life of the Brain* (New York: Houghton Mifflin Harcourt, 2017).

95   *Gregory Bateson*: see his influential essays in *Steps to an Ecology of Mind* (New York: Ballantine, 1972). I develop this point more fully in David Oates, *Paradise Wild: Reimagining American Nature* (Corvallis, OR: Oregon State University Press, 2003), 111–12 and throughout.

95   *100 billion neurons … "exceeds the number of known particles"*: Daniel J. Levitan, *This is Your Brain on Music* (New York: Dutton, 2006), 85.

95   *"Consciousness is more like music than computation"*: Dr. Stuart R. Hameroff, Director, Center for Consciousness Studies, University of Arizona, Tucson. http://quantumconsciousness.org/

96   *"almost savage"*: "Scherzo," in *Concise Oxford Dictionary of Music* (New York: Oxford University Press, 1980), 566.

VERMEER AND REMBRANDT

104   *Peter Schjeldahl*: "Vermeer," in *Let's See: Writings on Art from the New Yorker* (London: Thames and Hudson, 2008), 157–59.

106   *Vermeer's Milkmaid*: Johannes Vermeer, *The Milkmaid*. 1657 or 1658, oil on canvas. Amsterdam, Rijksmuseum.

108   *The Astronomer*: Johannes Vermeer, *The Astronomer*. c. 1658, oil on canvas. Paris, Louvre.

108   *The Lacemaker*: Johannes Vermeer, *The Lacemaker*. 1669–1670, oil on canvas. Paris, Louvre.

UMPTEENTH BRUMAIRE

115   *we can think beyond our cultural conditioning*: my point being that *of course* we are conditioned, and yet neither deaf to, nor immune from, the real world around us. See Oates, *Paradise Wild*, 138–41.

115 *rewrite history under the noses*: the precise quote is "rewriting contemporary history under the eyes of those who witnessed it." Hannah Arendt, "Truth and Politics" in *The Portable Hannah Arendt*, ed. Peter Baehr (NY: Penguin, 2000), 564. [Originally 1967.] I discuss this in the essay "Forgiving the Present (in Three Tries)," in David Oates, *What We Love Will Save Us* (Portland, OR: Kelson Books, 2009), 40.

116 *"The Eighteenth Brumaire of Louis Napoleon"*: Marx's periodical essay of 1852, eventually published as a small book. Collected in *The Marx-Engels Reader*, 2nd. ed., ed. Robert C. Tucker (New York: Norton, 1978), 594–617.

117 *half the peasantry and all the bourgeoisie*: "the reddest [i.e., most leftist] departments of the peasant population voted openly for Bonaparte" (Marx, 610), joined by the bourgeoisie which "now had no choice" but to do likewise (614).

118 *What seems overthrown*: Marx, 597.

118 *An entire people*: Marx, 596.

118 *insurance companies, which have embarked on a festival of self-enrichment*: Especially at first, Obamacare enriched health insurance companies: Paul R. La Monica, "Thanks, Obamacare! Health insurer stocks soar" (CNN Money, 21 January 2015). http://money.cnn.com/2015/01/21/investing/unitedhealth-earnings-obamacare/

119 *Every demand . . . stigmatised as "socialism"*: Marx, 602.

SEHNSUCHT AND THE DEEP PRESENT

120 *"Blau ist ein Lockvogel"*: Johanna Hansen, *Dasselbe Blau: Gedichte und Bilder* (Bad Bergzbern: Vinscript Verlag, 2013), 3. "Blue Is a Decoy" is my translation, by permission of the author.

122 *Bach's music carried me*: Johanna Hansen, "Briefwechsel zwischen Düsseldorf und Portland/Oregon," *Wortschau* (June 2015): 26. Trans. Dagmar Vossen.

THE POCKET SUBLIME

126 *To see a World in a Grain of Sand*: "Auguries of Innocence," in *The Poetry and Prose of William Blake*, 4th ed., ed. David V. Erdman (Garden City, NY: Doubleday, 1975), 481. This poem is not one of the "Songs of Innocence" but from a fair copy of additional work unpublished in William Blake's lifetime.

126 *What's the use*: See, perhaps, Dana Gioia, *Can Poetry Matter: Essays on Poetry and American Culture* (Saint Paul, MN: Graywolf Press, 1992).

127 *lyric magnitude*: the term belongs to M.H. Abrams, "Structure and Style in the Greater Romantic Lyric," in *From Sensibility to Romanticism: Essays Presented to Frederick A. Pottle*, eds. Frederick W. Hilles and Harold Bloom (New York: Oxford University Press, 1965), 527–60.

127 *To make a prairie*: poem number 571 in Emily Dickinson, *Final Harvest: Emily Dickinson's Poems*, ed. Thomas H. Johnson (Boston: Little, Brown, 1961), 319.

127 *The god of the small and the near*: my adaptation of the anonymous Aztec "Lord of the Close and the Near," which delighted my soul upon discovering it in an anthology for undergraduates, *Heath Anthology of American Literature*, vol. A, 5th ed., eds. Paul Lauter *et al.* (Boston: Houghton Mifflin, 2006), 89.

127 *"If I feel physically as if the top of my head were taken off . . .."*: Dickinson letter to Thomas Wentworth Higginson, qtd. in Thomas H. Johnson, "The Vision and

Veto of Emily Dickinson," *Final Harvest: Emily Dickinson's Poems*, ed. Thomas H. Johnson (Boston: Little, Brown, 1961), x.

128 *Ink whose body is a river*: Robert Sund, "The Table I Keep," in *Poems from Ish River Country* (Washington, DC: Shoemaker Hoard/Poet's House Trust, 2004), 216.

128 *The evening light fades through the clouds*: Robert Sund, "April has Turned Cold," 205.

129 *Somewhere in this ink bottle*: Robert Sund, book jacket.

CY TWOMBLY: DO NOT SAY

131 Twombly, Cy. *Achilles Mourning the Death of Patroclus*. 1967, oil on canvas. Paris, Le Centre Pompidou.

READING IN PARIS

133 *Václav Havel*: Václav Havel, *Disturbing the Peace* (New York: Vintage, 1991).

133 *Rich's book of essays*: Adrienne Rich, *What Is Found There: Notebooks on Poetry and Politics* (New York: Norton, 1993).

134 *"if all we would speak is ideology"*: Adrienne Rich, *The School among the Ruins* (New York: Norton, 2004), 47.

134 *"but who at the checkout"*: Rich, *School*, 48.

135 *Our dilemma is simple*: modified from Barry Lopez, *Resistance* (New York: Vintage, 2004), 10, 21.

135 *"will it matter if our tenderness"*: Rich, *School*, 71.

135 *James Baldwin*: for the record, it was *Go Tell It On the Mountain* (1953), which I picked up at Shakespeare and Company.

135 *Flaubert, his novel*: Gustave Flaubert, *Sentimental Education* (*L'Éducation sentimentale*). [Originally 1869.]

135 *"is how to bear witness"*: Adrienne Rich, *What Is Found*, 115.

135 *"privately and in secret"*: Rich *What Is Found*, 57.

135 *"[T]hese thoughts and feelings, suppressed"*: Rich, *What Is Found*, 57. Emphasis added.

136 *Havel's classic essay*: "The Power of the Powerless" (1978), in Václav Havel, *Living in Truth*, ed. Jan Vladislav (London: Faber and Faber, 1986), 36–122.

136 *"the distance between language and violence"*: Rich, *What Is Found*, 181ff. [Chapter title.]

136 *"The profound crisis of human identity"*: Havel qtd. in Rich, *What Is Found*, 162. Emphasis in original.

137 *"And in the end, is not the grayness"*: Havel, "Power," 54.

137 *"hunger for truth"*: Václav Havel, *Disturbing the Peace* (New York: Vintage, 1991), 183.

137 *"most portable . . . most concentrated"*: Rich, *What Is Found*, 124–25.

137 *"On my volcano"*: Dickinson qtd. in Rich, *What Is Found*, 93.

138 *"second culture". . ."hidden sphere"*: Havel, "Power," 101.

138 *"Under the orderly surface"*: Havel, "Power," 57.

138 *"opposition is every attempt to live within the truth"*: Havel, "Power," 73.

138 *"struggle to expand the space"*: Havel, "Power," 105–06.

138 *"every good piece of work"*: Havel, "Power," 81.

138 *"teachers . . . clergymen . . . painters"*: Havel, "Power," 87.

139 *"that must be taken hostage". . ."terrorized, sterilized"*: Rich, *What Is Found*, 125.

139 *"barbaric"*: the full quote is given in Rich, *What Is Found*, 141: "after Auschwitz, to write a poem is barbaric."

139 *"surely the Holocaust itself"*: Rich, *What Is Found,*141.

PICASSO: PUBLIC AND PRIVATE

140 *Le Perle*: found at Number 78 rue Vieille du Temple, if you're looking for a nice pub.

140 *Russell Martin . . . Picasso's War*: Russell Martin, *Picasso's War: The Destruction of Guernica and the Masterpiece That Changed the World* (New York: Dutton, 2002).

140 *Gernika*: the Basque spelling of the village. For his painting title, Picasso used the Spanish spelling.

141 *overweening tower . . . neighboring Nazi pavilion*: Martin, 106–08.

141 *"torpid indifference"*: Martin, 113–14.

141 *"Guernica saw only the backs of our visitors"*: qtd. in Martin, 121.

141 *"replaced by an artwork that made a stronger statement"*: Martin, 120.

141 *"lip-service"*: Martin, 204.

141 *refused to publicly denounce Franco*: Martin, 19.

141 *"believed he could do little"*: Martin, 73.

142 *The artist's canvas is the smallest of public squares. It is the Public Realm*: For this insight I am indebted to commentary by the curator Sara Antónia Matos at the exhibition of João Tabarra's photography (Gulbenkian Museum, Lisbon, February 12–May 18, 2014):

> This is perhaps the most daring and politically oriented proposal that art can effectively put forth: inviting each of us to take up a critical position on the world that we inhabit, constructing our subjectivity within it. Subjectivity is not limited to itself but exists in confronting others, in other people's suspicion that "a subject resides in me". . . Affirming these personal positions, making them public, equates to raising them into the domain of politics—to the *ágora*, in the Greek sense—a setting that belongs or should belong to all of us. This means that, in sharing positions of a private nature, in presenting them in the form of images, the artist confronts spectators with them and allows them to identify with these positions, leading them to perceive that experience itself, their inner narratives, could contain a political dimension . . .
>
> João Tabarra's images are constructed in such a way as to generate ambiguous situations and paradoxes and particularly to embrace a critical attitude, a space for judgment, which begins precisely with inner questioning and disquiet. In this respect, the poetic and the political operate alongside each other in João Tabarra's work; the public and the private intersect in unpredictable ways under a stain of suspicion.

143 *Christian Zervos . . . organized a double issue*: Martin, 122.

143 *Painting is not done to decorate apartments. It is an act of war*: Picasso qtd. in Martin [epigraph, n.p.].

143 *Picasso also writes our letter of doom:* Michel Leiris qtd. in Martin, 124.

143 *There is surely another world. But it is in this one:* Paul Eluard is mentioned by Martin as one of Picasso's observing friends during this time (122). But this well-known quote attributed to Eluard proves hard to source. I found a suspiciously vague online attribution to Eluard's *Œuvres complètes*, vol. 1, (Gallimard, 1968) [no page], giving this quotation (I've used my own translation): *Il y a assurément un autre monde, mais il est dans celui-ci.* According to John Llewelyn, *Margins of Religion: Between Kierkegaard and Derrida* (Indiana Univ. Press, 2008), 307, various sources perhaps misattribute this quote to Eluard: including Morris Berman's *The Reenchantment of the World* and Patrick White's *The Solid Mandela.* But Llewelyn finds an Eluard passage that offers the same gist, though of much greater wordiness.

ST. EUSTACHE III: SOLIDARITY AND THE SUBLIME

153 *there really is no such thing as society:* The exact quote from Margaret Thatcher is, "They are casting their problems at society. And, you know, there's no such thing as society. There are individual men and women and there are families. And no government can do anything except through people, and people must look after themselves first. It is our duty to look after ourselves and then, also, to look after our neighbours." Attributed to "an interview in *Women's Own* in 1987" in "Margaret Thatcher: A Life in Quotes," *The Guardian*, April 8, 2013. http://www.theguardian.com/politics/2013/apr/08/margaret-thatcher-quotes.

154 *Hayden White:* "The Politics of Historical Interpretation: Discipline and De-Sublimation," *Critical Inquiry* 9 (1982), rpt. in *The Critical Tradition: Classic Texts and Contemporary Trends*, 2nd ed., ed. David H. Richter (Boston: Bedford, 1998): 1297–1316.

155 *the "Soft Left" versus the "Hard Right":* Jack Dion, "La gauche molle contre la droite dure, c'est l'horreur politique," *Marianne*, January 30, 2014. http://www.marianne.net/La-gauche-molle-contre-la-droite-dure-c-est-l-horreur-politique_a235446.html.

155 *Paul Piff . . . Dachner Keltner:* "Why Do We Experience Awe?" *New York Times*, May 22, 2015, Sunday Review. This research is formally reported as Paul Piff et al., "Awe, the Small Self, and Prosocial Behavior," *Journal of Personality & Social Psychology*, 108.6 (2015): 883–99.

156 *Piff and Keltner. . . the tendency of wealth to reduce compassion:* described in Daisy Grewel, "How Wealth Reduces Compassion," *Scientific American*, April 10, 2012. http://www.scientificamerican.com/article/how-wealth-reduces-compassion/.

157 *"[W]e suggest that people insist on experiencing more everyday awe":* Piff and Keltner, "Why Do We Experience Awe?"

Works Cited

Abrams, M. H. "Structure and Style in the Greater Romantic Lyric." In *From Sensibility to Romanticism: Essays Presented to Frederick A. Pottle,* edited by Frederick W. Hilles and Harold Bloom, 527–60. New York: Oxford University Press, 1965.

Adams, John Luther. *Winter Music: Composing the North.* Middletown, CT: Wesleyan University Press, 2004.

Arendt, Hannah. "Truth and Politics." In *The Portable Hannah Arendt,* edited by Peter Baehr, 545–75. New York: Penguin, 2000. [Originally 1967.]

Bachelard, Gaston. *The Poetics of Space.* Translated by Maria Jolas. Boston: Beacon Press, 1969.

Bacon, Francis. "Of Beauty." In *The Essays,* edited by John Pitcher, 189–90. New York: Penguin, 1985.

Baldwin, James. *Go Tell It On the Mountain.* London: Penguin, 1991. [Originally 1953.]

Barrett, Lisa Feldman. *How Emotions Are Made: The Secret Life of the Brain.* New York: Houghton Mifflin Harcourt, 2017.

———. "What Emotions Are (and Aren't)." *New York Times,* 2 Aug 2015, Sunday Review: 10.

Barrias, Louis Ernest. *Le Serment de Spartacus* (The Oath of Spartacus). Marble, 1869–1871. Jardin des Tuileries, Paris.

Basilique du Sacré Coeur de Montmartre. "The Origin of the Construction of the Basilica, a 'National Vow.'" http://www.sacre-coeur-montmartre.com/english/history-and-visit/article/the-origin-of-the-construction-of.

Bateson, Gregory. *Steps to an Ecology of Mind.* New York: Ballantine, 1972.

Baum, Nicholas, *The Mystery of Hieronymus Bosch.* BBC/Bayrische Rundfunk (televised film, nd.).

Behnke, Robert J. *Trout and Salmon of North America.* New York: Chanticleer, 2002.

Blake, William. "Auguries of Innocence." In *The Poetry and Prose of William Blake,* 4th ed., edited by David V. Erdman, 481. Garden City, NY: Doubleday, 1975.

Bosch, Hieronymous. *The Temptation of St Anthony.* Triptych, oil on wood panels, c. 1501. Lisbon, Museu Nacional de Arte Antiga.

Boulton, James T. "Introduction." In Edmund Burke's *A Philosophical Enquiry into the Origin of our Ideas of the Sublime and Beautiful.* Edited and introduced by James T. Boulton, xv–cxxvii. Notre Dame, IN: University of Notre Dame Press, 1968.

Burke, Edmund. *A Philosophical Enquiry into the Origin of our Ideas of the Sublime and Beautiful.* Edited and introduced by James T. Boulton. Notre Dame, IN: University of Notre Dame Press, 1968.

Denner, Balthasar. *Woman With a Blue Hood.* Oil on copper (1721–28). Paris, Louvre.

Dickinson, Emily. *Final Harvest: Emily Dickinson's Poems*. Edited and introduced by Thomas H. Johnson. Boston: Little, Brown, 1961.

———. *The Letters of Emily Dickinson*. Edited by Thomas Johnson and Theodora V. Ward. Boston: Belknap/Harvard University Press, 1958.

Dion, Jack. "La gauche molle contre la droite dure, c'est l'horreur politique." *Marianne*, January 30, 2014. http://www.marianne.net/La-gauche-molle-contre-la-droite-dure-c-est-l-horreur-politique_a235446.html.

Dixon, Laurinda. Review of Larry A. Silver, *Hieronymus Bosch* (New York: Abbeville Press, 2006). *Renaissance Quarterly* 60.2 (2007): 594–596.

Eliot, T. S. "The Dry Salvages." In *The Four Quartets*. Boston, New York: Houghton Mifflin, 1971: 39. [Originally 1943]

Flaubert, Gustave. *Sentimental Education*. London: Wordsworth, 2003. [Originally 1869 as *L'Éducation sentimentale*.]

Gibbs, Christopher H. *The Life of Schubert*. Cambridge: Cambridge University Press, 2000.

Gibson, Walter S. "Bosch's Dreams: A Response to the Art of Bosch in the Sixteenth Century." *Art Bulletin* LXXIV.2 (June 1992): 201–17.

———. Review of Daniela Hammer-Tugendhat, *Hieronymus Bosch: Eine historische Interpretation seiner Gestaltungsprinzipien* (Munich: Wilhelm Fink, 1981). *Art Bulletin* LXVI.1 (1984): 160–63.

Gioia, Dana. *Can Poetry Matter?: Essays on Poetry and American Culture*. Saint Paul, MN: Graywolf Press, 1992.

Grewel, Daisy. "How Wealth Reduces Compassion." *Scientific American*, April 10, 2012. http://www.scientificamerican.com/article/how-wealth-reduces-compassion/.

Hameroff, Dr. Stuart R., Director. Center for Consciousness Studies, University of Arizona, Tucson. http://www.quantumconsciousness.org/content/overview.

Hansen, Johanna. "Blau ist ein Lockvogel." In *Dasselbe Blau: Gedichte und Bilder*, 3. Bad Bergzbern: Vinscript Verlag, 2013.

———. "Briefwechsel zwischen Düsseldorf und Portland/Oregon." *Wortschau* (June 2015): 26. Translated by Dagmar Vossen.

Harris, Lynda. *The Secret Heresy of Hieronymus Bosch*. Edinburgh: Floris Books, 1995.

Havel, Václav. *Disturbing the Peace*. New York: Vintage, 1991.

———. "The Power of the Powerless." In Václav Havel, *Living in Truth*, edited by Jan Vladislav. London: Faber and Faber, 1986. 36–122. [Originally 1978.]

Jamme, Franck André. *Au Secret*. Plounéour-Menez (France): Éditions Isabelle Sauvage, 2010.

———. *To the Secret*. Trans. Norma Cole. New York: La Presse, 2015.

Johnson, Thomas H. "The Vision and Veto of Emily Dickinson." Emily Dickinson. *Final Harvest: Emily Dickinson's Poems*, edited by Thomas H. Johnson, vii–xiv. Boston: Little, Brown, 1961.

Kramer, Lawrence. *Franz Schubert: Sexuality, Subjectivity, Song*. Cambridge: Cambridge Univ. Press, 1998.

La Monica, Paul R. "Thanks, Obamacare! Health insurer stocks soar." *CNN Money*, January 21, 2015. http://money.cnn.com/2015/01/21/investing/unitedhealth-earnings-obamacare/.

Le Poidevin, Robin. "The Experience and Perception of Time." In *The Stanford Encyclopedia of Philosophy* (Summer 2015 Edition), edited by Edward N. Zalta. http://plato.stanford.edu/archives/sum2015/entries/time-experience/.

Levitan, Daniel J. *This is Your Brain on Music*. New York: Dutton, 2006.

Llewelyn, John. *Margins of Religion: Between Kierkegaard and Derrida*. Bloomington, IN: Indiana Univ., 2008.

Lopez, Barry. *Resistance*. New York: Vintage, 2004.

"Lord of the Close and the Near." In *Heath Anthology of American Literature*, vol. A, 5th ed., edited by Paul Lauter et al., 89. Boston: Houghton Mifflin, 2006.

Lyotard, Jean-François. "The Sublime and the Avant-Garde." In *The Sublime*, edited by Simon Morley, 27–40. London and Cambridge, MA: Whitechapel Gallery/MIT Press, 2010.

Martin, Russell. *Picasso's War: The Destruction of Guernica, and the Masterpiece That Changed the World*. New York: Dutton, 2002.

Marx, Karl. "The Eighteenth Brumaire of Louis Napoleon." In *The Marx-Engels Reader*, 2nd. ed., edited by Robert C. Tucker, 594–617. New York: Norton, 1978. [Originally 1852.]

Morely, Simon, ed. *The Sublime*. London and Cambridge, MA: Whitechapel/MIT, 2010.

"Mount Saint Helens." *New World Encyclopedia*. http://www.newworldencyclopedia.org/entry/Mount_Saint_Helens.

"Mount St. Helens, 30 years ago." *Boston Globe*. May 18, 2010. http://archive.boston.com/bigpicture/2010/05/mount_st_helens_30_years_ago.html.

Nicolson, Marjorie Hope. *Mountain Gloom and Mountain Glory: The Development of the Aesthetics of the Infinite*. New York: Norton, 1959.

Oates, David. "Forgiving the Present (in Three Tries)." In *What We Love Will Save Us*, 37–50. Portland, OR: Kelson Books, 2009.

———. *Paradise Wild: Reimagining American Nature*. Corvallis, OR: Oregon State University Press, 2003.

Ortega y Gassett, José. *Meditations on Hunting*. Trans. Howard B. Wescott. New York: Scribners, 1985. [Originally 1942.]

Piff, Paul, et al. "Awe, the Small Self, and Prosocial Behavior." *Journal of Personality & Social Psychology*, 108.6 (2015): 883–99.

———and Dachner Keltner. "Why Do We Experience Awe?" *New York Times*, May 22, 2015, Sunday Review.

Rich, Adrienne. *The School among the Ruins*. New York: Norton, 2004.

Rich, Adrienne. *What Is Found There: Notebooks on Poetry and Politics*. New York: Norton, 1993.

Sacks, Oliver. *Musicophilia: Tales of Music and the Brain*. New York: Knopf, 2008.

"Scherzo." *Concise Oxford Dictionary of Music*, 566. New York: Oxford, 1980.

Schjeldahl, Peter. "Vermeer." In *Let's See: Writings on Art from the New Yorker*, 157–59. London: Thames and Hudson, 2008.

Schiller, Friedrich von. *Naive and Sentimental Poetry and On the Sublime*. Translated and introduced by Julius A. Elias. New York: Frederick Ungar, 1966.

Shimelmitza, Ron, et. al. "'Fire at will': The emergence of habitual fire use 350,000 years ago." *Journal of Human Evolution* 77 (2014): 196–203.

Schroeder, William. "Balthasar Denner (1685–1749): Portrait Artist." *Mennonite Historian* 30, no. 1 (2004): 1–2.

Sedgwick, Eve Kosofsky. *Between Men: English Literature and Male Homosocial Desire*. New York: Columbia University Press, 1985.

Shepard, Paul. *Coming Home to the Pleistocene*. Edited by Florence Shepard. Washington, DC: Shearwater/Island Press, 1998.

———. *Nature and Madness*. San Francisco: Sierra Club, 1982.

———. *The Tender Carnivore and the Sacred Game*. New York: Scribner, 1973.

Silver, Larry A. "God in the details: Bosch and Judgment(s)." *Art Bulletin* 83.4 (Dec 2001): 626–650.

Solomon, Maynard. "Franz Schubert and the Peacocks of Benvenuto Cellini." *Nineteenth-Century Music* 12.3 (1989): 193–206.

———. "Schubert: Some Consequences of Nostalgia." *Nineteenth-Century Music* 17.1 (1993): 34–46.

Stevens, Wallace. "Sunday Morning." In *The Palm at the End of the Mind: Selected Poems and a Play*, edited by Holly Stevens, 5–8. New York: Vintage, 1972. [Originally 1915.]

Sund, Robert. "April has Turned Cold." In *Poems from Ish River Country*, 205. Washington, DC: Shoemaker Hoard/Poet's House Trust, 2004.

———. "The Table I Keep." 216.

Thatcher, Margaret. "[A]n interview in Women's Own in 1987." In "Margaret Thatcher: A Life in Quotes." *The Guardian*, April 8, 2013. *http://www.theguardian.com/ politics/2013/apr/08/margaret-thatcher-quotes*.

Twombly, Cy. *Achilles Mourning the Death of Patroclus*. Oil on canvas, 1967. Paris, Le Centre Pompidou.

Van Gogh, Vincent. *Fritillaries in a Copper Vase*. Oil on canvas, April–May 1887. Paris, Musee D'Orsay.

Vermeer, Johannes. *The Astronomer*. c. 1658. Oil on canvas. Paris, Louvre.

———. *The Lacemaker*. 1669–1670. Oil on canvas. Paris, Louvre.

———. *The Milkmaid*. 1657 or 1658. Oil on canvas. Amsterdam, Rijksmuseum.

Viola, Bill. *The Quintet of the Astonished*. 2000, Color video rear projection, 15:20 minutes. Paris, Grand Palais.

de Voragine, Jacobus. *The Golden Legend*. Translated by William Granger Ryan. Princeton, NJ: Princeton University Press, 1993.

White, Hayden. "The Politics of Historical Interpretation: Discipline and De-Sublimation." *Critical Inquiry* 9 (1982). Rpt. in *The Critical Tradition: Classic Texts and Contemporary Trends*, 2nd ed. Edited by David H. Richter, 1297–1316. Boston: Bedford, 1998.

Word Reference (Dutch). www.wordreference.com/nlen